First Edition

Written by Sara and Shannon Burns
Design by Marilyn Burns and Nick Burns
Photos by Sara and Shannon Burns

To contact Burns Family Studios write to
info@beyondthemaskmovie.com

For further information, visit www.burnsfamilystudios.com
or www.beyondthemaskmovie.com

ISBN-13: 978-0-9968050-0-1

BEYOND THE MASK

The Official
Illustrated Movie Guide

Sara and Shannon Burns

BURNS FAMILY STUDIOS PRESENTS "BEYOND THE MASK" ANDREW CHENEY KARA KILLMER ADETOKUMBOH M'CORMACK SAMRAT CHAKRABARTI STEVE BLACKWOOD AND JOHN RHYS-DAVIES MUSIC BY JURGEN BECK DIRECTOR OF PHOTOGRAPHY ETHAN LEDDEN COSTUME DESIGNER MARILYN BURNS PRODUCTION DESIGNER NICK BURNS EDITED BY MIKE WECH CASTING BY BEVERLY HOLLOWAY, CSA ACTING COACH JOHN KIRBY SCREENPLAY BY PAUL MCCUSKER WITH STEPHEN KENDRICK AND BRENNAN SMITH ASSOCIATE PRODUCER TRACEY BURNS CO-PRODUCED BY CHAD BURNS PRODUCED BY AARON BURNS DIRECTED BY CHAD BURNS

BeyondTheMaskMovie.com

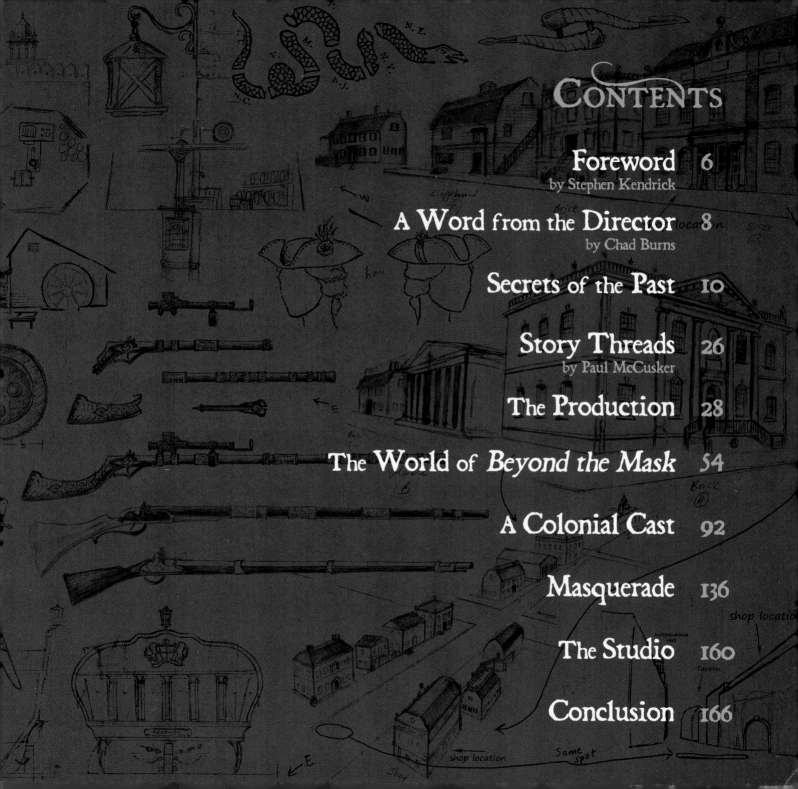

CONTENTS

Stephen Kendrick
FOREWORD

Over the last few years, my brother Alex and I have met countless filmmakers who exude vision and passion and are astute with some of the latest digital technology. It is refreshing, however, to find those rare jewels who also have hearts that passionately beat for God and are willing to attempt great things in cinema for His glory. I believe this is true of Chad and Aaron Burns and their team at Burns Family Studios.

I've had the privilege of getting to know these men and their families over the last three years. It has been a joy to watch them grow as Christ-followers and filmmakers and to interact with them during each leg of their journey with the movie *Beyond the Mask*. As they first demonstrated on *Pendragon*, they aren't afraid to dream big, trust God, and relentlessly carry a massive project to completion.

There are many special things about *Beyond the Mask* that have set it apart in my mind. It has a very unique premise—that what we are and can accomplish on our own is empty and vain compared to the surpassing greatness of knowing Christ and being found in Him. When was the last time you saw an action-adventure love story about that? When I read the first few pages of the script, I wanted to see this movie become a reality.

Secondly, it is a historically based period piece that required a large percentage of the wardrobe, sets, props, and vehicles to be designed and built from the ground up. This was no small undertaking, and the Burns family pulled it off by God's grace on a small budget. Thirdly, this movie probably has more green-screen shots and CG effects than almost any other live-action Christian film in history.

The real adventure has been their creative climb of that digital Everest. Fourthly, I know that *Beyond the Mask* was covered in prayer. Major decisions, needs, and problems were addressed with intercession. That's my passion, and I believe God will honor them for making prayer more than a token tagalong.

But beyond the uniqueness of the movie, I've seen unique things about this team that have made me want to keep cheering them on. While most filmmakers are dying to make a name for themselves, this team has sought to die to themselves to make a movie that lifts up Christ's name instead. Their focus and humility have been refreshing. Their willingness to seek and receive the tough counsel of others has been commendable (Proverbs 12:15). Before the script was completed, they wisely set up a board of godly advisers to counsel and hold them accountable during each stage of the journey. This was a grand-slam decision on multiple levels. I believe that all of these things are a recipe for something great.

With all this in mind, this wonderful book the Burns family has developed chronicles the faithfulness of God and lessons learned throughout the production of *Beyond the Mask*. I join in their excitement of what God might do through the exciting journey of Will and Charlotte and I pray that He chooses to bless and mightily use this movie and team for His glory.

Grateful to be found in Him,

Stephen Kendrick
Cowriter, Producer
Facing the Giants, Fireproof, Courageous, War Room

"I count all things to be loss in view of the surpassing value of knowing Christ Jesus my Lord, for whom I have suffered the loss of all things, and count them but rubbish so that I may gain Christ, and may be found in Him, not having a righteousness of my own derived from the Law, but that which is through faith in Christ, the righteousness which comes from God on the basis of faith."

PHILIPPIANS 3:8-9 NASB

Chad Burns

A WORD FROM THE DIRECTOR

Making *Beyond the Mask* was a journey that the Lord used to shape my life. The production effort for myself and my business partner, Aaron, spanned three years. In that time I finished my education, fell in love and married, lived with my wife at five locations in two states, and saw the birth of our first child.

Beyond the Mask was many things. It was a little lake next to the apartment where we lived in Champaign, Illinois. My wife and I would often go there to recover after disappointing meetings with would-be investors. There were days, and weeks that stretched into months, where the future of BTM was uncertain. We didn't have the money we needed to make the film, and the doors were not opening. Each meeting felt like asking a girl out on a first date, and most of them were saying no. But then, in God's own time, the financing came together.

Beyond the Mask was camaraderie—the feeling of accomplishment and elation when you know that as a team you have created something wonderful. When you know that you would never look back and say I wish we had pushed for one more shot, because as a team you pushed to the very limit of physical endurance. That feeling of being very alive but so dead tired.

Beyond the Mask was the opportunity to work with a group of people who dreamed an impossible dream and then woke to make it happen. It was sharing fellowship around a meal, and around the Word, and in song. It was the banjos playing long into the night outside our bedroom door; it was the guys cheerfully taking cold showers with a hose in the front yard when the sewers backed up. It was

thrilling emotional performances, great stunts, amazing sets, new friends, new places, new challenges. It has been our life.

Beyond the Mask has also been our reminder. It is a story about a man who seeks his identity and justification through the things that he does. It surprises me how often I slip into the trap of desperately desiring to find myself, my hope for tomorrow and my purpose for today, in a job well done, in a film well liked, in a project well executed.

There are two reasons why finding our identity this way will never work. First, because there is a cosmic sense of disappointment. Even in the best things that we do, the groans of a broken world are always lurking around the edges, reminding us with a melancholic sense that we have fallen short. Second, it has been truly said, "Art is never finished, only abandoned." This is true of the many things we pursue but feel unable to totally finish. Together, these facts lead us eventually to an inescapable sense of loss for what could have been. They make finding identity in our work, even excellent work, a disappointing pursuit.

That's the bad news. Fortunately, there is also good news. Nothing in this world was meant to satisfy us or to leave us with the feeling of true completeness or wholeness. Jesus gives us Himself for this, saying, "I am bread, I am living water." On the cross He groaned once for all, so that one day we might know Him face-to-face and lay aside our groaning forever. To the extent we have the sense of falling short, it is because we have. It is in Him that we can finally stop being insufficient as we accept His amazing resume in place of our own short efforts. If we feel we must abandon our work, it is because we must—He graciously finishes the work in our hearts and finishes the work in this world with His return and re-creation. We are not meant to finish the task, only to trust and follow hard after Him for our season.

Beyond the Mask was three extraordinary years of my season, an adventure which I was tremendously privileged to be a part of. It was an opportunity to take risks and live larger in a gospel-centered sort of way. I hope you will enjoy reading this book, which captures the journey through the pictures and stories of the people who lived it.

The story of Will Reynolds is the story of us all—a man looking to find the identity that will make him complete and fix the deep problems he carries with him. He will discover that he must abandon his own efforts to achieve this and rest instead in the finished work of Christ.

Chad Burns
Director, *Beyond the Mask*

Secrets of the Past

Political Spotlight
1776

The dawn of 1776 found the American colonies at a pivotal point in history. The colonies were torn between those who remained loyal to their English sovereign and those who struggled for freedom. War had already broken out in Massachusetts, and George Washington was in the field commanding the colonial forces. Across the continent, newspapers were filled with the injustices of unfair taxation, the forced quartering of troops, and judges who answered to the crown. Blood ran hot in Philadelphia as delegates of the Continental Congress debated dissolving their ties with England. The cry for independence was in the air.

Amidst this struggle, former assassin William Reynolds finds himself in Philadelphia, drawn by the girl he loves and the man he loathes. He cares nothing for the king and fights not for independence, but instead wages his own private war against Charles Kemp, the man who robbed him of his future and even his name. Kemp, an official of the East India Company, takes advantage of the colonies' unrest to gain power.

While William Reynolds and Charles Kemp are fictitious, the world they live in is not. The year 1776 is known to all Americans as the year we proclaimed our independence from England, but few know what was happening beyond the political spotlight.

PREVIOUS PAGE: The East India Company's logo.

OPPOSITE: A prison ship lies at anchor in a New York harbor.

ABOVE: A loyalist mob stirs up trouble in the streets of Philadelphia.

A Colonial Superpower

THE EAST INDIA COMPANY

On the night of December 16, 1773, the stillness of Boston was shattered by the war whoops of patriots loosely disguised as Indians. The sounds of splintering crates and the splash of tea being hurled into Boston Harbor filled the air. The men knew that this was an act of rebellion against the king, but the crown was not the only power that the patriots defied that night. The crates of tea that bobbed in the harbor were the property of a mighty force in the global economy—the East India Company. This company was responsible for 15 percent of all exports to Britain—the most powerful kingdom in the world. Domineering and ruthless, the Company held a tyrannical rule over its holdings in India. But with resources in the East running dry, they turned a greedy eye on the American colonies.

> "a *mighty force*, with the power to mint *money*, to command *fortresses* and *troops*, to form *alliances*, and to exercise both civil and criminal jurisdiction"

The East India Company began in the year 1600 with a small group of merchants who saw the potential for trade in the Indies. These enterprising gentlemen convinced Queen Elizabeth I to grant them a royal charter, giving them a trade monopoly extending from the Cape of Good Hope, east to the rising sun. The vast and untapped potential of the Indies lay before them.

The dawn of 1647 found the Company with twenty-three factories spread out across the East. They now held influence in Surat, Madras, Bombay, and Calcutta. With their interests expanding, the Company gained influence in the British political realm, and around 1670, the king granted the Company full control over their holdings. They were given the power to mint money, to command fortresses and troops, to form alliances, to make war and peace, and to exercise both civil and criminal jurisdiction over the acquired areas. The East India Company had become an empire.

But this empire's rule was not benevolent. Famine broke out in the region of Bengal, due in large part to the Company's insistence that the

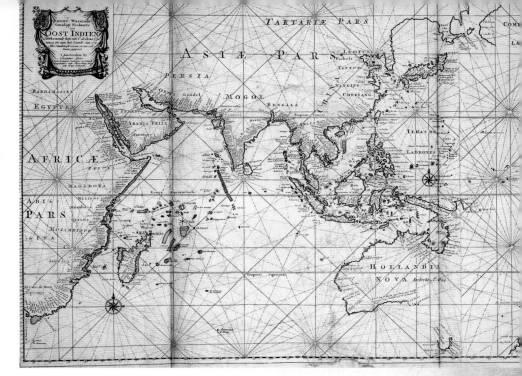

OPPOSITE: Trading ships from around the world filled the harbors of the Indies.

RIGHT: An old map of the East Indies.

inhabitants plant large amounts of opium and indigo for export instead of the region's staple food—rice. By 1770, one-third of the population had died. Caring nothing about the destruction they had caused, officers who had grown rich in India began to move back to England and establish large estates for themselves.

Alarmed by reports of the Company's corrupt rule of their territories, Parliament stepped in. England's legislature passed several new laws attempting to take more control over the Company's business dealings. Trade was slackening, and debts began to mount. Hoping to gain new territories with fresh potential, the East India Company turned to the American colonies. In 1773 Parliament granted them greater influence in the American market through the Tea Act. Excited by new trade opportunities, the Company sent eight million pounds of tea to be sold in the already turbulent colonies. As news of the Tea Act spread, fear and indignation boiled in its wake. The people of the colonies knew that this was not a goodwill offering from the crown. Looking at the destruction in India, they rightly feared what the East India Company had planned for America.

The East India Company plays an important part in the story of *Beyond the Mask*. As the film begins, William Reynolds is an assassin employed by East India Company executive Charles Kemp. Will is haunted by his misdeeds in Asia, and although he wants to put his former life behind him, the Company's evil plans follow him to America. There he is forced to get involved yet again in Company politics.

BELOW: Starting with the original EIC logo (FAR LEFT), *Beyond the Mask's* concept artists created the version of the logo that appears in the film, personalized with Charles Kemp's initials.

1

2

3

THE
EAST INDIA
COMPANY

"They have levied War, excited Rebellions, dethroned lawful Princes, and sacrificed millions for the sake of gain. The revenues of mighty Kingdoms have centered in their coffers. And these not being sufficient to glut their avarice, they have, by the most unparalleled barbarities, extortions and monopolies, stripped the miserable inhabitants of their property, and reduced whole provinces to indigence and ruin . . . They now, it seems, cast their Eyes on America, as a new theatre, whereon to exercise their talents of rapine, oppression and Cruelty. The monopoly of tea, is, I dare say, but a small part of the plan they have formed to strip us of our property."

John Dickinson was one of America's Founding Fathers and was present at both the Continental Congress and the Constitutional Convention. He frequently penned political letters, identifying himself as a farmer. The excerpt above is from Dickinson's 1773 work: "A Letter from the Country to a Gentleman in Philadelphia." Here Dickinson outlines the East India Company's past atrocities and his grave concerns about its plans for America.

The Real Assassin
PLOT AGAINST WASHINGTON

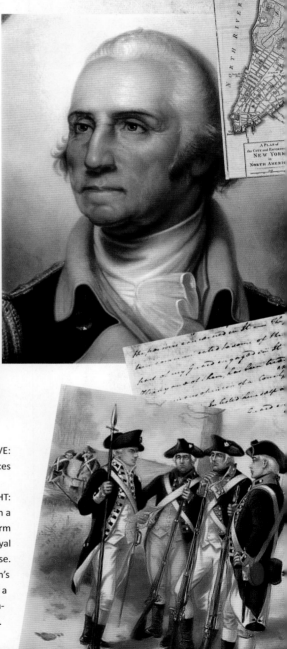

In 1776, the young country had more to fear than the king's army: the land was filled with British sympathizers known as Tories. The Tories' underground networks tried to recruit the citizens around them and overthrow the Continental Congress. The most notable of their schemes was the plot to assassinate General George Washington. At the center of this plot were influential men including the British governor of New York and New York City's mayor. These men had a wide range of subordinates, but their best asset was a man in Washington's own bodyguard.

This deadly plan was uncovered and reported by a certain Samuel Fraunces. Fraunces was born and raised in the Indies, arriving in America in his early thirties. During the Revolution, Fraunces aided the Sons of Liberty and may even have been a spy for the colonials. When he uncovered the plot against Washington, Fraunces was put in a colonial prison due to the belief that he was one of the conspirators. He was later acquitted of any wrongdoing. Undaunted, the Tories remained active with a new plot to destroy New York's defenses, and the revolutionaries were once again working to stay one step ahead of their subtle enemies.

Woven into the film is the New York attempt on Washington's life. Much like Fraunces, Will Reynolds has a past in the Indies and is framed while trying to expose the true conspirators.

Washington's firsthand account of the assassination attempt: *"The plot had been communicated to some of the Army and part of my Guard engaged in It—Thomas Hickey, one of them, has been tried and by the unanimous opinion of a Court Martial is sentenced to die."*

ABOVE:
Samuel Fraunces

RIGHT:
Not every soldier in a continental uniform was completely loyal to the rebel cause. One of Washington's own guard had a hand in the assassination plot.

Alan Madlane

BEN FRANKLIN

Every American is familiar with the face of Benjamin Franklin, so finding an actor who could portray him was quite a challenge. When the Los Angeles casting call did not reveal any options, the team opened up country-wide video auditions but were still at a loss. Just weeks before filming was scheduled to begin, Alan Madlane caught the attention of the casting team when he came in to audition for the role of Richard Harrison. They were impressed with his abilities as an actor. But he was not Richard Harrison. Alan had already left the room when the casting team had the idea to have him try out for the part of Franklin. Caught just as he was exiting the building, he was brought back into the audition room and asked to read for the new role. Given only an hour to prepare, Alan delivered from memory four pages of Franklin's dialogue and stole the part.

Beyond the Mask is set in 1776, so Benjamin Franklin would have been about seventy years old, with the familiar balding hairline that can be seen on the one-hundred-dollar bill. Alan was far younger than the aging Franklin, but he was willing to be transformed into this well-known politician. The hair and makeup team had to shave the top of Alan's head, gray his hair, and add extensions for length. That was the simple part. To age his face, lead makeup artist, Bree Shea, spent three hours applying prosthetics to his skin to give it a realistic wrinkled texture. This extensive routine had to be repeated each morning before he arrived on set, giving Alan the longest time in hair and makeup of any actor

It was important that Madlane have the distinctive look of Ben Franklin (pictured at right).

BEN FRANKLIN – *Printer, Scientist, Politician*
COLONIAL TECHNOLOGY

Everyone has heard stories about Benjamin Franklin, the witty delegate from Pennsylvania. Who isn't familiar with his quip "Early to bed, early to rise, makes a man healthy, wealthy, and wise"? His wit and his genius have won him a lasting place in the hearts of the American people—but did you know . . .

Franklin was apprenticed to his older brother James at the age of twelve to be taught the trade of printing. In 1730, at twenty-four, Franklin went into business for himself and began publishing *The Pennsylvania Gazette*. The *Gazette* gave Ben a platform to share his opinions about the growing unrest and the outcry for freedom in the colonies. His paper became the first to publish political cartoons, among them the famous sketch of the snake saying "Join or Die." Franklin officially retired from the printing

> " *He* who would give up a little *Liberty* for *Security* deserves neither and loses both."
>
> *B. Franklin*

business in 1748, although he continued to publish the *Gazette*. After quitting the press, he spent his years as a philosopher, politician, and inventor. Yet, even with his many other accomplishments, Franklin always considered himself a printer by trade.

The tale of Franklin flying a kite during a thunderstorm is one of the best known stories of his life as an inventor. But few know that his work with electricity went far beyond kites and keys. At that time, many scientists were fascinated by electricity, but few understood it. In 1774 the concept of catching an electrical charge was exploited by

ABOVE: Franklin's historic political cartoon.

a German scientist who created the Leyden jar. A Leyden jar is a glass jar lined with metal and then charged with electricity. The charge is created by an electrostatic generator, which is made up of two major components: a glass plate that is spun by hand and a set of wire brushes. The brushes rub on the spinning plate and create static electricity, which runs down wires to the Leyden jar, where it is caught and stored by way of two separated chemicals—much like a modern double-A battery. Franklin discovered that he could link Leyden jars in a series, resulting

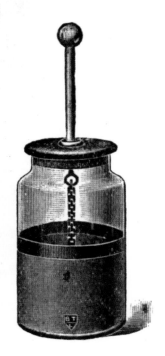

in a much larger charge. This discovery he called a battery, setting its name for years to come.

Franklin was a member of the Continental Congress and part of the committee that wrote the Declaration of Independence. But that was not the only committee on which he served. In 1775, the Committee of Secret Correspondence was created, and Ben, along with four others, was appointed to head the effort. These men directed a spy ring, providing lines of communication between the revolutionaries and their spies in Great Britain. The committee also created codes and cyphers, directed operations of agents abroad, and secretly bought munitions for the army. Through the Committee of Secret Correspondence, and in his role as the first American ambassador to France, Franklin worked to turn influential people on the world stage to favor American independence.

Franklin enters Will Reynolds's world when he hires Will on as a new employee in his Philadelphia print shop. His political involvements as well as his inventions play an important role in the film.

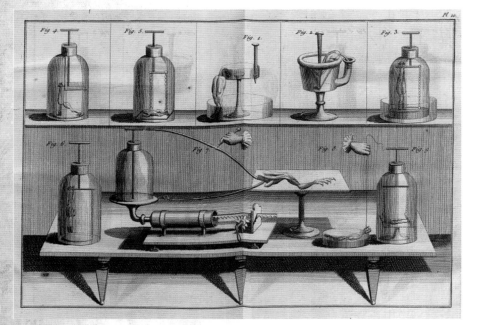

ABOVE: A Leyden jar. Next to his political work, Franklin is best known for his fascination with electricity.

LEFT: Leyden jar diagrams

OPPOSITE: The electrostatic generator's Leyden jars from *Beyond the Mask*. (INSET) Replicas of Franklin's Leyden jars in a museum display.

Fact or Fiction?
WINDMILL ISLAND

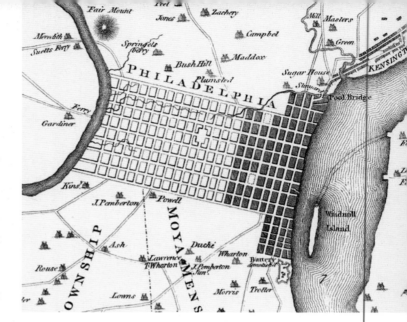

For many years, a tiny island stood in the Delaware River, in view of the city of Philadelphia. Shrouded in mystery, it had its origins in a shipwreck that took place sometime before the 1600s. The vessel was never pulled from the river, and as the years went by, silt collected around the debris. By 1746, it had formed a small island.

In that year, the island fell into the possession of John Harding and his son, who found it large enough to build a windmill. The island derived its name from this structure and was simply called Windmill Island. Only sketchy details are available about Harding, although it appears his windmill was used to process grain. At low tide, sandbars appeared that linked the island to the mainland, allowing horses to cross with their sacks of grain. At some point, a storm swept down the river and blew the top of the windmill off the island. From that point on, aside from being the site of several executions, Windmill Island seems to have been deserted until 1838, when a channel was cut through it to allow the passage of ferryboats. The new, smaller island this created was called Smithes Island, and it became a weekend recreational location for the citizens of Philadelphia. Taverns and pavilions popped up as the site gained popularity. But in 1894, the islands were deemed a shipping hazard and were dredged out of the river. A fascinating discovery was made when the

ABOVE: An old map of Philadelphia clearly shows Windmill Island's location in the Delaware River.

LEFT: Artist's depiction of Windmill Island built on the wreckage of old ships.

OPPOSITE: (TOP) Concept art of the abandoned windmill. (BOTTOM) Sketch depicting how the future set would appear.

islands were being cleared from the river: the old wrecked ship's hull was still there, only nine feet from the surface. Today nothing is left of Windmill Island, leaving only questions behind.

These facts are the framework on which the *Beyond the Mask* crew created the details of Charles Kemp's electro-static generator chamber. Built underneath Windmill Island in the hull of the old sunken ship, Kemp's chamber offers one explanation for the windmill's intended purpose and the mysteries surrounding it.

An EAST PROSPECT of the CITY of PHILADELPHIA; taken by GEORGE HEAP from the JERSEY

A DESCRIPTION of the SITUATION, HARBO

under the Direction of NICHOLAS SCULL Surveyor General of the PROVINCE of PENNSYLVANIA.

OF THE CITY AND PORT OF PHILADELPHIA.

ABOVE: *Beyond the Mask's* Windmill Island was based on a sketch of Philadelphia Harbor from the 1700s (LEFT). Note the presence of Independence Hall and Windmill Island in the sketch.

Paul McCusker
STORY THREADS

*P*aul McCusker is a writer and director for the beloved *Adventures in Odyssey* radio series with its host of classic characters. "We grew up listening to Paul McCusker's stories, so you can imagine how excited we were to have the chance to work with him on the screenplay for *Beyond the Mask*," says producer Aaron Burns. Paul is also known for his work in adapting classics such as Dickens's *A Christmas Carol* and *The Chronicles of Narnia* by C.S. Lewis for Focus on the Family's Radio Theatre. He is a prolific writer who has authored forty novels. "It was a privilege to bring such a distinguished writer onto our team," says Aaron. From the budding story that Aaron and Chad brought to him, Paul wove a masterpiece. The characters and dialogue in *Beyond the Mask* belong to Paul.

LEFT: Paul McCusker, cowriter and director of *Adventures in Odyssey*.

BELOW: Odyssey characters Eugene Meltsner and Connie Kendall.

FOCUS ON THE FAMILY
RADIO THEATRE®

How I came to be a part of the writing team
Paul McCusker

A mutual friend suggested that Chad and Aaron Burns should contact me about writing a screenplay for them. Frankly, I was a bit skeptical. For one thing, I often hear from people who want to make films and want me to write screenplays—and nothing comes of the offers. For another, I anticipated that these two gents wanted to make another "kitchen table" drama with domestic conflict about marriage or family issues. I do a lot of that kind of writing in my day job, so I wasn't excited by the thought of writing that kind of film. I agreed to a phone call but was prepared to say a "thanks but no thanks."

Then I learned that the Burns boys had actually made a film, which had earned some money (unheard of), and that it was an ambitious historical fantasy drama called **Pendragon.** *So I had to revise my thinking and expectations as I went into the call.*

First impressions are important—and my first impression of Chad and Aaron was that they were enthusiastic, creatively ambitious, and passionate about producing something more than your average "Christian" drama. They immediately dispelled my concerns about their ability to do what they planned to do. And then they pitched the idea about this East India tea mercenary in 1775 who gets betrayed, winds up seeking revenge during the backdrop of American independence, but finds something else along the way. The whole conversation was so unexpected that I felt compelled to say yes.

The real work began after that, as we took their premise and began the arduous process of turning it into a story that would fulfill their intentions. We did the storyboard process and worked out a basic story arc—and then reworked it again and again as the characters, who were vague notions of themselves at the start, became flesh and blood with their own motivations and passions. We argued over theology. We debated how to take an essentially spiritual idea—which is very internal and often works against the format of film—and make it work for an action-adventure. We struggled with good ideas, even excellent ideas, that we had to let go of because they didn't really fit as well as they needed to. We fought over plausibility versus imagination, historicity versus artistic license, plot versus theme. In other words, we did all the things that have to be done to create a movie.

Chad and Aaron were saintlike in their patience as I rambled on and around and through and in and out of whatever subject we had to tackle. Both men were gracious but remained tenacious in their vision. They knew what they wanted and stayed on track to see it realized.

I think the hard part came with the compromises we had to make because of budget and time. I'm still thinking that I should write a novel of the film if only to recapture all the stuff we wanted to do, but couldn't.

But the harder part, which we knew from the beginning, was in weaving a theme of redemption into the film without it feeling forced or implausible. The nuances of bringing a character to a recognition of spiritual need, in a way that would resonate with the audience, hung over us through every part of the process. And now we watch to see if we succeeded.

Paul maps out the *Beyond the Mask* plot.

THE PRODUCTION

THE PRODUCTION TEAM

It takes a massive network of people to create a film, and *Beyond the Mask* was no exception. Each detail in the movie—from the intricate embroidery on Charlotte's dress to the soaring music in the soundtrack—had a team of individuals behind its creation. At every stage of production, there were teams of people working to bring *Beyond the Mask* to the screen. Although most of the production work on the film was done in Michigan, only a handful of these people were from that state. The crew was made up of people from states as far away as California, Texas, and Oregon, and the team even included people from Canada, India, and Germany. Their backgrounds varied as well. Many of the department heads were seasoned professionals in their fields, but a few had only a handful of films under their belt and were eager new recruits, bringing their energy and fresh perspectives to the project. On the pages that follow, you will have the opportunity to meet a few members of the crew that made *Beyond the Mask*.

PREVIOUS PAGE: A crew member stands in for Andrew Cheney as the G&E team rigs a 12x12 silk on Chestnut Street to diffuse the harsh sunlight.

RIGHT: Filming begins on the exterior of Franklin's shop.

Chad Burns
DIRECTOR

"*A*lthough a director has many jobs, most of them would fall under the 'creative management' label," director Chad Burns says. "The specific jobs of a director can range from writing out initial ideas for a film to location scouting, auditions and casting, working with actors on set, and overseeing creative development of individual departments.

"Principal photography, or production, is the shortest phase of filmmaking, although it is ironically what most people associate with 'making a movie.' As the director, it is my job to work with the first assistant director (first AD), who is my on-set coordinator, to keep the production team rolling. I am also the person working with the talent to craft their performance and make sure that the story is being clearly told through them.

"In a practical way, I have been involved in making short films with family members since I was a kid. Our first foray into filmmaking was a short film about a superhero clash. This later led to longer films, commercial films, and eventually our first feature: *Pendragon: Sword of His Father*. But it wasn't until grad school for engineering that filmmaking caught my attention as being a viable career. I spent time studying engineering but found what I enjoyed most were opportunities for team leadership and managing projects. My desires at this season of my life were shifting. I was feeling the Lord move my heart as He opened the door to plunge into filmmaking in a serious way.

"On *Beyond the Mask* I was primarily directing the actors on set and working with department heads beforehand to establish a look and feel. Once we got to shooting, the first AD and DP (director of photography) took care of most of the shot-related items while I focused more on the performances. I'd arrive on set with the DP and first AD and other department heads a couple hours before picture up. We'd talk over the shots and sometimes hand out sides or storyboards. Problem areas would be identified and discussed. Art would give us an update on the set, which if we were at a new location, might still be under construction. I'd then work with the actors for on-set rehearsals. That's how the mornings usually went."

Without the producer, the crew was lost. Department heads would come to Aaron with impossible dilemmas on a daily basis, and with his phone and his faithful office staff, he would always turn out a solution.

OPPOSITE: Aaron pauses to take a photo with actress Kara Killmer on the Chestnut Street set.

Aaron Burns
PRODUCER

"*A* producer is ultimately responsible for organizing and managing every aspect of the film's production. This includes everything from initial story ideas all the way to postproduction and distribution," says Aaron Burns, producer of *Beyond the Mask*. "As producer, it's your job to fix problems of every kind, and you're always doing that with limited resources. So producing is a challenging job and one I really enjoy.

"What really led me into producing was watching the response to our first film—*Pendragon: Sword of His Father*. After we released it domestically to DVD, we started receiving hundreds of letters from the families who watched it—parents telling us that *Pendragon* was their kids' favorite movie and kids saying that it had a big impact on their lives. Opportunities opened up for us to release it internationally, and *Pendragon* was dubbed into three additional languages and is for sale around the world. The thought that this movie was having an impact for the Lord and encouraging people across the globe while I was here in Michigan was really exciting to me. It made the challenges and risks of what we were trying to do worthwhile.

"Chad and I were excited about the opportunity to make another period, Christ-centered action-adventure film on this scale. It was my job to figure out how to fit the massive scope of the project into a budget, determine where to focus our resources, and build a team of people who would rally around a unique project like this. Producing *Beyond the Mask* has been an adventure. We got a chance to work with explosions, sword fights, horses, muskets, and secret technology. We were able to film in some amazing places like Scripps Mansion, the Henry Ford Museum, and Crossroads Village. And we got to fly in professional actors from all over North America and John Rhys-Davies from the UK. Every one of these elements brought its own set of unique challenges but also made the project a lot of fun to work on!"

Chip Lake
MAKING IT HAPPEN

Chip Lake was the assistant director on *Beyond the Mask*. "As AD, my role is to work closely with the director and the DP (director of photography) to help them execute their vision for the film. I figure out what they want to do and then make it happen," Chip explains. "I think of my job like the hub of a spoke wheel. All the spokes of production run to me, and my job is to hold them all together so that the wheel can turn smoothly.

"I went through the script and broke it down into the details of what was needed for each shot—the actors, the props, the equipment, and so forth. Next, I developed a shooting schedule that fit the demands of the project.

I worked for over two weeks to figure out the schedule for the production of *Beyond the Mask*: how we could shoot it under all the restraints we had. Then I determined the number of days we needed to shoot the movie.

"My role during production was to keep the movie going in a forward direction. I made sure that the people in props, wardrobe, camera, etc. were getting the information they needed about the upcoming schedule. I also kept tabs on all the departments to make sure that their stuff was ready on set when it was needed. Essentially, my job was to make sure the crew met their goals, on time and on budget."

Production Office		BEYOND THE MASK	CALL SHEET	
Production Office			DATE: **Wednesday, Oct 10, 2012**	
Ortonville, MI 48462		See individual call times on back	DAY: **29 of 48** BREAKFAST: 3:20 PM	
Phone: Production Office		**4:00 PM**	SHOOTING CALL: **5:30 PM**	
Producer: **Aaron Burns**			1st MEAL: 10:00 PM to 10:30 PM	
Director: **Chad Burns**			2nd MEAL: 4:00 AM to 4:30 AM	
1st AD: **Charles Lake**			WRAP: **4:00 AM**	
Associate Producer **Tracey Burns**		Set medic: John Hedrick •	Weather: Partly cloudy and windy. 20% chance of morning shower; clear night	
UPM: **Andrew Bolzman**			**High: 49 • Low: 34**	
No Forced Calls or OT Without Prior Approval by Production		Current Script Version: Pink rev. 10/6/12	Sunrise: 7:41 AM • Sunset: 7:00 PM	
		Current Schedule Version: Buff2 rev. 10/7/12		

PLEASE BE PRESENT AND READY TO GO BY YOUR CALL TIME
** VIDEO VILLAGE IS A WORK AREA. ESSENTIAL PERSONNEL ONLY. **

Scenes	Sets & Descriptions	Cast/Ward#	D/N - SD	Pages	Locations/Notes
39pt4	EXT - CHRIST CHURCH OF HOLLOWAY "He will come to us."	2, 7 / CK2, B1	D - 14	2/8	
8pt3	INT - KEMP HOUSE - STUDY Reynolds meets Kemp to discuss future	1, 2, 7 / WR2, CK1, B1	N - 2	2 4/8	
83pt2	EXT - PHILADELPHIA - KEMP HOME Charlotte and Will meet on veranda Kemp interupts	2, 3 / CK4, CH11	N - 30	4/8	**Scripps Mansion**
43pt3	INT - LIVERPOOL - EAST INDIA COMPANY OFFICE Weapons chamber - Sees Franklin's name	1 / WR10	N - 14	1/8	
43pt4	INT - LIVERPOOL - EAST INDIA COMPANY OFFICE Weapons chamber	1 / WR10	N - 14	0/8	
43pt2	INT - LIVERPOOL - EAST INDIA COMPANY OFFICE Reynolds sneaks through EIC hallway, up elevator, staircase	1 / WR10	N - 14	2/8	
8pt2	INT - THE KEMP MANOR HOUSE-HALLWAY STUDY Reynolds walking down hallway with Basil	1, 7, 54, 55 / WR2, B1	N - 2	1/8	
	All Schedules Subject to Change		**Total Script Pages =**	**3 6/8**	

ID	Cast	Character	Status	Pickup	Call	Block	MU/Ward.	Set	Remarks
1	Andrew Cheney	Will Reynolds	W	5:00 PM	5:15 PM	-	5:15 PM	6:30 PM	Pickup
2	John Rhys-Davies	Charles Kemp	W	4:05 PM	4:20 PM	-	4:20 PM	5:15 PM	Pickup
3	Kara Killmer	Charlotte	W	7:00 PM	7:15 PM	-	7:30 PM	11:00 PM	Pickup
7	Samrat Chakrabarti	Basil	W	4:05 PM	4:20 PM	-	4:20 PM	5:15 PM	Pickup
54	Henri Franklin	Kemp Bodyguard 2	SWF	self	10:00 PM	-	11:30 PM	12:30 AM	Self drive
55	Leroy Williams	Kemp Bodyguard 1	SWF	self	10:00 PM	-	11:30 PM	12:30 AM	Self drive

BACKGROUND & ATMOSPHERE

#	Description	Report	Set call	Scenes
-	-	-	-	-
-	-	-	-	-
-	-	-	-	-
-	-	-	-	-
-	-	-	-	-
-	-	-	-	-
-	-	-	-	-
-	-	-	-	-
-	-	-	-	-
-	-	-	-	-
-	-	-	-	-
-	-	-	-	-
0 = *Total Extras*				

SPECIAL INSTRUCTIONS

SET DRESSING:	Charles Office Decor-A3, EIC wall Emblems, Large Desk, muskets (6), weapons cabinet
PROPS:	3 menards 4x8 brick pannesl, 4 real brick panels, Charles' cane, flint-lock tripwire, Official Document Envelope , Oil Lantern LED, Ornate Indian jacket, Random official files- I1, Random papers- i1, reynold's cane, Sniper Rifle (WILL REYNOLDS), tattered threads, pins, and scraps of maps and charts
MAKEUP/HAIR:	
WARDROBE:	B1 (BASIL), CH11 (CHARLOTTE), CK1 (CHARLES KEMP), CK2 (CHARLES KEMP), CK4 (CHARLES KEMP), WR10 (WILL REYNOLDS), WR2 (WILL REYNOLDS)
SFX:	Hazer, 2 Cloth 10x20 GS, Tailored Foam GS
CAMERA:	
GRIP/ELECTRIC:	
SOUND:	
LOCATION:	Scripps - Back porch, Dining room, Hallway, Library, Stone Walls
WEAPONS:	Firing Muskets 8, Firing Pistols 3
STUNTS:	
ANIMALS:	None

ADVANCE SCHEDULE - Thursday, Oct 11, 2012

Scenes	Sets & Descriptions	Cast	D/N - SD	Pages	Locations/Notes
87	EXT - MAYOR'S HOUSE - PATIO William exposed!	1, 2, 7, 13, 17, 26, 38 43	N - 31	4 1/8	**Scripps Mansion**

NEXT 7 SEVEN DAYS AT A GLANCE *(times are estimates)*

Thu, Oct 11	Fri, Oct 12	Sat, Oct 13	Sun, Oct 14	Mon, Oct 15	Tue, Oct 16	Wed, Oct 17
4 PM to 4 AM	4 PM to 4 AM	4 PM to 4 AM	OFF	OFF	7 AM to 7 PM	7 AM to 7 PM
Scenes: 87	*Scenes: 84*	*Scenes: 86*	*None*	*None*	*Scenes: 104, 106, 52pt1*	*Scenes: 109, 113pt1, 45pt1, 45pt2*

1st AD: Charles Lake	Producer: Aaron Burns

OPPOSITE: Directing the extras' action is one of the many jobs of the assistant director. Here Chip outlines the path for the colonial soldiers to march.

RIGHT: A call sheet is a schedule for a specific shooting day that is created by the assistant directing team. It contains information such as the crew's call time, the day's shooting location, and the weather forecast.

Ethan Ledden
CAPTURING THE IMAGE

"The DP (director of photography) is responsible to capture the director's vision for the given scene and to communicate that look to the gaffer and the grips so they know where the lights are to be set up to get the given look, whether it's supposed to be dramatic or light or dark."

Ethan has been involved with Burns Family Studios since 2006 as the studio's director of photography. In the early stages of developing their first feature film, *Pendragon*, the studio sent out DVDs with a trailer to a number of filmmakers. Ethan received one of these packages and contacted Chad. He and his brother, Dustin Ledden, joined the project and have continued to work on the studio's productions.

Using light to tell the story, the DP has to be specific about the depth, light, and shadow of the image being captured in the camera. "We can enhance the light, happy feelings with lighter, less shadowed, more glowing light, and enhance the darker moods with shadows. But it had to look good enough that no one would think about the way it was lit; they would just watch it and be drawn in and wouldn't ever be distracted by the lighting.

"One thing that struck me on this project was just how much production design comes into play with the lighting. Almost just as much as you are working hand in hand with the gaffer, you are working with the production design people. Because if they can't get you details in certain places, you can't paint with the light. So it's almost like a triangle with the production design people. Whenever I got a chance to plan with the art team, and help it work together with the lighting, it made for even better material.

"The fact that *Beyond the Mask* was a period piece and had a lot of unusual material to work with was really nice, because we weren't just shooting in ordinary houses and living rooms. It made it a lot easier to create footage that looked really nice, because there was so much production value going into it. It makes a DP's job so much easier when he's already got intriguing things to work with and he just needs to make it look good."

ABOVE: Ethan operates the Red Epic camera. This is the same camera that Peter Jackson used to shoot *The Hobbit*.

OPPOSITE: Cameras A and B on the Windmill Island set.

LEFT: This shot is being filmed OTS (over the shoulder), while the second camera shoots the scene clean, or without any foreground objects.

LEFT: The shape of the camera changed every day depending on which attachments the camera team needed to get the shot.

RIGHT: To film the carriage bomb explosion sequence, the carriage was jacked up in front of a green screen. Just before the camera turned on, the wheels were spun and the fuse was lit. The camera was wrapped in protective cloth to shield it from the explosion's flying sparks.

RIGHT: An external monitor was attached to the camera for the first AC (assistant camera) to work from. The scene came to life when viewed through the monitor. No one on set had the same perspective as the camera.

Brent Christy
LIGHT IT UP

On a film crew, the gaffer designs the lights to make the scene look the way the director of photography has envisioned. He has a team of grips (the G&E team) working with him to position each lighting element in its place. Brent is a brilliant gaffer who has worked on over sixty films, including *Iron Man 3*.

"I got into filmmaking when I was working at a television station, and that is where I got an interest in working with a camera. And then from there it [was] just a progression of meeting new people, going to college, and finding out that lighting was something that really interested me. I'm from Michigan, and I moved back to Michigan not long after college when the [film] incentives were booming. There were many new crew members, and I fell into the ranks and got experience."

There were many impressive lighting setups on the project, but two stood out to Brent as his favorites. The first was the proposal scene at the front door of Scripps Mansion. "It was a very emotional moment, and we were able to do a lot of fun lighting that brought some emotion to the scene. I really enjoyed that . . . Over the first few weeks of production, they kept showing the scene to the crew on a laptop. It was fun to see it in a rough edit so quickly and show everybody the results of the hard work that they put in. Another favorite scene was one we shot against a green screen with the actors in a boat inside the [studio warehouse]." In story space, Will and Charlotte are in a boat at night, rowing down the Delaware River. When the scene was filmed, however, the crew was inside the studio warehouse with a cement floor underneath the boat instead of water. This meant that the lighting team had to convince the audience of the exterior setting with the light. "We had an effect for the water and an effect for the rocking boat. Those are the two situations that stood out to me as the most fun to wrap our heads around."

ABOVE: Lighting equipment in hand, Brent stands ready on set.

BELOW: Holes were cut in the roof of the generator room set, and blue lights shone inside to simulate sunlight filtering through water.

TOP: View of the interior of the generator room with the blue light streaming in from the roof.   ABOVE: Still from the final shot.

Each shot on a cinema camera must be manually focused by the first AC. It isn't always convenient to reach the camera's focus ring. Here Brent Christy supports Alex Lerma as he hangs out over the water in order to reach the focus ring.

OPPOSITE: (TOP LEFT) One of the many tasks in a grip's job description is positioning the heavy lighting equipment.

(TOP RIGHT) Nathaniel Brunner and Timothy Jones wave branches and flags in front of the lights to simulate the movement of shadows as the carriage drives along a wooded road.

(BOTTOM LEFT) Will's room in Franklin's attic was built as a three-walled set with no roof, allowing the lighting crew more space to work.

(BOTTOM RIGHT) The G&E team rigged their largest green screen in the film for the ship set.

Dustin Ledden
FIRE, WATER AND STUNTS

"As special effects supervisor, I worked out how we were going to shoot the effects. Say we had to swing people from rafters. My job was to figure out how we were going to do it logistically, how the stunt was going to be done safely, and whether we could use the real actors or if we needed to use stunt doubles," Dustin Ledden, the special effects supervisor says. "So, as my title implies, I co-ordinated the effects and then I supervised them.

"One thing about *Beyond the Mask* was the scope. It is continent-spanning, so that meant that there were a lot of interesting things to try to figure out about how and what we were going to shoot. This played into the style of fighting that we had in the film. We looked at some Indian martial arts, but they did not fit the look of the film, so we went with a Filipino martial art style instead. We also incorporated some stick fighting, and there is a good deal of just brawling mixed in too."

Dustin was in charge of choreographing all the fights in the movie. "We had thirteen to eighteen fights or actions to be choreographed in *Beyond the Mask*. The fight between Will and Joshua inside the vicarage was something like 120 moves. I would write down all the moves for a fight, and then I would run through those moves with a stand-in to check the flow and visual appeal before I would teach them to the actors."

RIGHT: Dustin was the staff scuba diver and water safety patrol—always in the water whenever an actor was swimming for a shot. He also operated an underwater camera for several scenes.

BELOW: Will's stunt double jumps from the bridge to the roof as he takes Windmill Island by storm.

OPPOSITE: (LEFT) Will dispatches a guard who stands in his way as he flees the church.

(RIGHT) Dustin and Andrew work through the moves for the final sword fight between Will and Basil.

SUGAR GLASS

Over the course of the film, forty panes of breakaway glass were hand-crafted by special effects assistant Aaron Ledden. With its razor edges, real glass was obviously too dangerous for a stuntman to dive through, so breakaway glass had to be used. After hours of experimentation, Aaron perfected a mixture to create an imitation glass. By using Isomalt and burnt sugar, he made the brown stained glass for the church window. This imitation glass was very sensitive to temperature and melted quickly. Due to its fragility, the glass was never made until the night before it was needed, requiring Aaron and his assistants to spend many sleepless nights "cooking" glass.

BELOW AND RIGHT: Three versions of the large bay window in Franklin's shop had to be made. The first was created from Plexiglas, the next was the sugar glass stunt window, and the third was a shattered Plexiglas window.

A chain of crew members use a rope and pulley system to hoist Andrew and Kara up out of the elevator shaft.

BELOW LEFT: The stunt team often used cardboard boxes as extra cushioning for stunt landing pads.

BELOW RIGHT: Will's stunt double jumps between "rooftops."

ABOVE: A stuntman holding a dummy plays the highwayman rescuing a girl from a burning house. This was an indoor, daytime scene filmed outside at night. A large wall was constructed to create a flaming backdrop for the stuntman as he kicked his way out of what appears to be a flame-engulfed room. The shot was captured in slow motion to accentuate the flames.

OPPOSITE: (TOP) Will's and Charlotte's stunt doubles dive into the water, followed closely by a flaming windmill blade being controlled by crew members offscreen. Dustin monitors safety from the water.

(BOTTOM) The crew stands by as the art department preps the fire effect. Keeping fires and torches burning throughout the night was a full-time job. Fog machines added atmosphere to the surroundings.

Jurgen Beck
WRITING MUSIC FOR AN EPIC

"I don't create music, I create emotions," explains composer Jurgen Beck. "The music partners up with the story and the visuals and cinematography to achieve that."

Music adds great depth to a film's storytelling. Jurgen compares a soundtrack to the narration in a novel: "There's more time [in a book] to really go into what the characters are thinking about. In a film, music takes some of those qualities, from an emotional perspective, and adds them to what is actually on the screen. For *Beyond the Mask*, what that means is, music has the opportunity to tell some of the backstory."

In order to transport his audience into the film's historical setting, Jurgen dove into Colonial Era music, look-

"I sketch and often orchestrate the music with the pen display, in addition to pencil and paper. It is a beautiful modern-day way of drawing directly on the screen."

OPPOSITE: One of Jurgen's handwritten sketches of the score.

Photo courtesy of Jurgen Beck.

ing to discover clues about musical phrasing, the types of instruments available, and other details. "You can't load up the score with a bunch of synthesizers, like what you would hear in a modern-day action film," he says. "So it adds to the challenge." The careful listener can pick out period instruments such as the pennywhistle, auto-harp, zither, and field drums, adding a layer of texture and realism to the score. These elements from the eighteenth-century world are interwoven into the cinematic score.

Location is another part of the story that Jurgen gets to tell. "We do have a fairly wide span of locations that all require a little bit of a different take on music," he says. As the plot crosses oceans, from the American colonies to Mother England to India and back, the musical themes reflect the changes of scenery and culture. "We do have the East India Company as a prominent offscreen character, if you will. We're telling the story of both Kemp and Will in their own dealings with the East India Company. So quite naturally, we introduce instruments that are authentic to that location to convey the feeling that, yes, now we're in India."

The final story element in the score is that this is an epic tale, and that means music that makes a big sound. "Very early on, we decided that we would allow the music in the film, the musical signature, to be very, very large. We're looking at an expansive [story] with a range of styles, dates, and locations that allows for that. It provides that perfect platform for that very large cinematic, symphonic sound. That's just a great challenge, and I tremendously enjoy that."

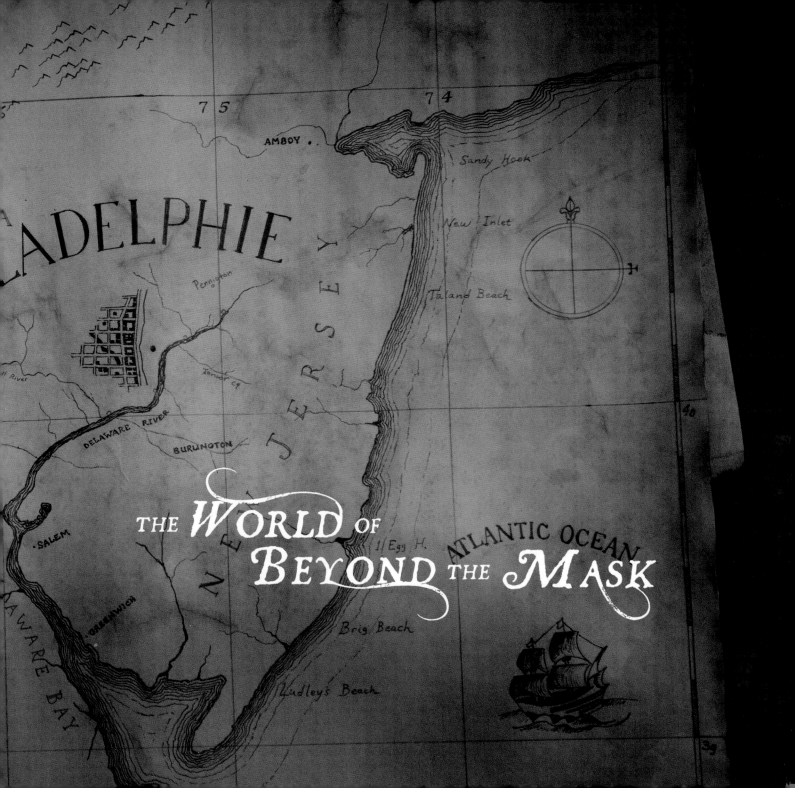

THE *WORLD* OF
BEYOND THE **MASK**

BUILDING A WORLD

*I*t was the job of the production design team to recreate eighteenth-century Philadelphia, London, and other locations for *Beyond the Mask*. Whether it was an extensive city street or a simple bedroom, each set contributed to making a believable and historical world. Whether it was the weave of brick on the storefronts or the color of paint on the walls, every detail was carefully constructed to help draw the audience into the story, taking the viewer back to the 1700s.

Burns Family Studios needed a production lot. This would be a location hub that would provide the facilities for the team as well as a place to build the sets. The team prayed about this need, and God answered beyond what they had expected. Hillside Bible Church had purchased a piece of land to use as a future building location but was willing to let the film crew use it. This property was on a main road and had three barns, a two-story farmhouse, a pond, and some vacant fields. This became the production lot for the project. Much of the crew boarded in the farmhouse. The catering team cooked out of the kitchen. The main pole barn became the studio warehouse. And seven main sets were built at the location.

The environments the art team created provided a dynamic space in which the actors could work. Creative and ingenious, the art team seemed never to run out of energy. Working within the limits of a very short preproduction schedule, the teams completed seven main sets in record time.

The crew prepares to film on the Windmill Island set. The structures stood twenty feet high with the top of the set extended in postproduction.

ABOVE: Extras bring the Philly set to life.

RIGHT: A sketch of Chestnut Street's layout.

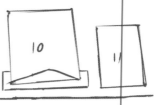

CHESTNUT STREET

The 1700s found the city of Philadelphia a bustling port city. Two-story brick shops lined the streets, and ships filled the harbor. In the middle of it all ran Chestnut Street. Close to Independence Hall and Benjamin Franklin's little print shop, this section of the city was a critical location both in American history and the *Beyond the Mask* story.

The Philadelphia street set was the only reproduction set that the *Beyond the Mask* art team had to create. There are many sketches and paintings from the time, and much of the original city of Philadelphia is still toured, so it was important that this set be laid out correctly as well as look historically accurate. "We spent a great deal of time figuring out where Independence Hall would be in relation to the street, where the harbor would be, what direction you would be looking down the street if you stood at the harbor and looked toward Franklin's print shop, and where the taverns would have been," production designer Nick Burns says.

Nick researched colonial styles and immersed himself in the architecture of the time. He studied what Chestnut Street looked like and how the front of Franklin's shop would have appeared. Franklin's original shop was destroyed, and a replica now stands on the property. The team visited the site and pulled together sketches, paintings, and descriptions from the 1770s to recreate an accurate look for the shop. It was originally three stories tall, but the art team decided to build one-and-a-half stories and add the remaining height of the shop in postproduction.

RIGHT: The steadicam operator runs to keep up with Will as he dashes through the streets of Philadelphia.

LEFT: The print shop's door and window frames were made almost entirely of Styrofoam.

BELOW: The tunnel next to Franklin's shop was lined with eight panels of Styrofoam bricks

CENTER: Nick's sketch showing the building's dimensions.

OPPOSITE: (TOP) Each brick had to be measured and traced on individually to ensure that the panels lined up correctly.

(MIDDLE) The Styrofoam panels were screwed onto plywood fronts in the studio backlot.

OPPOSITE: (BOTTOM) The art team repurposed the print shop by repainting and adding an awning.

Creating all of the bricks for the houses and shops along the street was one of the main tasks in front of the team. It was out of the question to use real bricks because of their weight, so they had to make false brick panels. Although it is possible to buy premade brick panels, they are not made with the correct colonial weave, which is called Flemish bond. "We really didn't want the building to take on what I call a 'schoolhouse' look, where you see the really orange bricks that are all the same size and in the classic weave," Nick says. "So we opted to make our own bricks. This way we were also able to add a great deal of depth and unique weathering to the bricks that we would not have been able to find if we had gone with a processed panel." The art team made brick panels from 4'x8' pink insulating Styrofoam boards. Transforming the panels was an intensive process. First each board had to have the bricks measured and drawn on,

after which the grout lines would be melted in using wood burners, which left raised bricks. Next the panel would be distressed with a

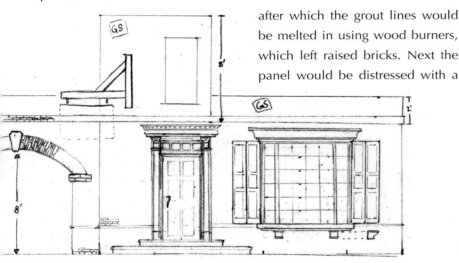

wire brush, to give it a porous look, and then it was pounded with stones to destroy the perfectly flat surfaces of the Styrofoam. This gave the bricks a more random and almost wavy appearance. Next, three coats of paint went on. The first was a dark gray base; next, tan in the grout lines; and lastly, mixtures of brown and red. Each individual panel took twelve hours to complete. Recreating Chestnut Street took a massive amount of work, but the final result was quite incredible and well worth the effort.

VISUAL EFFECTS

*T*he world of *Beyond the Mask* was not only built with hammers, nails, and Styrofoam: the extensive scope of many of the sets was created using digital effects. The film contains 750 VFX shots, which translates to 65,000 frames, making one out of every three shots in the film an effect. That's fifty minutes of playtime!

Designing the digital effects was an enormous task and required a team of skilled artists to accomplish. Aaron explains the team dynamics: "We had thirty artists in North America and Europe, as well as teams in India and Nepal. So our team was working around the globe, around the clock. We used a software tool called Shotgun, which is like Facebook for VFX artists. It allows a constant stream of feedback and input for each shot. Compared to everyone being on set together, camaraderie can be lacking with a team working remotely, so we got creative: we decided to throw some virtual parties. At Christmas, we had a virtual party where everyone from the team ordered pizza, reviewed some of the shots, and chatted on a Google Hangout. So no matter where you were located, it was a fun opportunity to pull the whole team together."

The process of taking recorded footage and creating digital elements to populate it had several stages. Many of the shots began with characters on a partial set in front of a green screen. "The shot would go to our rotoscoping team first," Nick, who was also on the matte painting team, says. "They would carefully cut out the green screen, and then our matte artists would create the background with 2-D digital matte paintings. In many shots we also used 3-D elements combined with the matte paintings to give us the best look.

Then each of those layers would be given to a compositor, who would put it all together and render out the final shot."

The team did an incredible job, and as the final product shows, they successfully completed a colonial world for Will Reynolds to bring to life.

ABOVE: A 3-D colonial storefront.

OPPOSITE: Three still frames show the progression from original footage to a test composite to the final image. Because the camera was on a dolly running down the street, this shot had to be match-moved. In a match move, software is used to track points in the footage and recreate the camera's path through the environment.

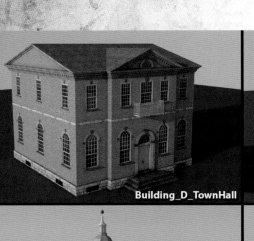

Building_D_TownHall

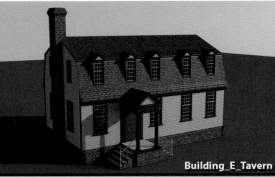

Building_E_Tavern

Building_C_Gad Tav

Building_G_CourtHouse

Building_H_Bank

Building_I_Chu

Building_J_Apartment

Building_L_Mill

Building_M_Apartm

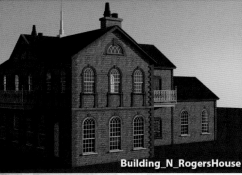

Building_N_RogersHouse

Building_P_AaronsHouse

Buillding_O_ChadBurnsHo

OPPOSITE: Many of the 3-D buildings created for the rooftop chase scene were based on photographs of existing historical structures. Each detail, from the shutters to the porch railings to the crown molding, had to be recreated to reflect colonial architecture. Once these models were placed into the shot, a matte painter would add details such as shadows, dirt, or grunge to make them look more realistic.

Director Chad Burns was set on having a classic colonial house in the film, and he requested such a specific look that when designers created a model to his specifications, they dubbed it "the Chad Burns House" (pictured in the bottom row).

LEFT: A version of the rooftop chase with rough modeling blocked in was produced for the director to review.

The rooftop chase sequence was one of the most complex visual effects sequences in the entire film, containing thirty-six shots. In a computer-generated environment, details such as dust, moisture, smoke, and fog have to be added to the scene, but those final atmospheric elements often take the shot from fake to realistic. (Opposite Top) Concept art of the rooftop chase sequence. (Above) This is a screen capture from the program *Cinema 4D*, which was used to build the 3-D models in *Beyond the Mask*.

KEMP'S OFFICE

*T*he production designer wanted an Indian flare to be mixed into the affluence of an English manor house for Charles Kemp's office. Kemp earned his fortune working for the East India Company and spent many years in the South Asian regions before the story begins. The office décor reflected that influence, while the room itself remained clearly British. "We wanted this set to be large and impressive," Nick says. "We wanted Will to have to walk a ways before he reached Kemp's desk, and we wanted the desk to be large and intimidating." Scripps Mansion, a Tudor-style estate, was an expansive location used for several sets. The mansion's library was full of deep, rich woods, an ideal backdrop for this set.

"One of my favorite set pieces that we found at Scripps was Kemp's chair. The chair was large and made from very ornately carved wood. It was really way over the top, but that matched Kemp's personality well and represented not only his status in the company, but also his place in society."

LEFT: The art team removed all of the modern books and replaced them with muskets and Indian decor, so that even the shadows behind Kemp would remind the audience of his past.

His Majesty's ship, the *Colossus*.

SHIP

"The ship set took a colossal effort," Nick remembers. Initially, the team considered the option of renting a tall ship on Lake Huron to use for the set. But it soon became clear that it would be simpler, more cost-effective, and would actually look better to build one themselves. "As much work as it would be to build the rear and deck of a ship, it was going to be easier than trying to find a tall ship and work through all the logistics of remaking it into a 1770s vessel," Nick says.

The first blueprints for the ship showed the back of the ship and the deck as two separate sets. But when the ex-tank commander in charge of its construction wanted to build it as one piece, Nick said, "Why not?" So the set went from being on the ground to sitting on stilts fifteen feet in the air. "I think it was the right choice," Nick says, "because the ship became a complete set, and we were able to focus our set dressing all in one place. So it worked out well from a set design aspect." The construction manager for the set was well-versed in the layout and make of an historic seagoing vessel. Providing direction for the construction of the ship, his knowledge was a great help in pulling all the right pieces together and giving the set the authentic look that appears in the film.

TOP: The ship's deck was made of particleboard that was scored and painted to render planking.

MIDDLE: The crew works to finish the ship set with only six hours until filming begins.

BOTTOM: The art team does detail touch-ups, adding a layer of grunge to the set.

This one set serves as two different ships in the film. In the opening sequence, it is used as a British ship that William Reynolds and Joshua Brand raid. Later in the film, Charlotte meets Will on a colonial prison ship that is actually the same set remastered. The art department made the prison ship look old, neglected, and far from seaworthy, while the British ship carries the royal coat of arms on her stern and sparkles with a fresh coat of paint.

The art team dug a pool beneath the end of the ship in order to film Charlotte's tumble off the deck and into the New York harbor. A stunt double took the dive, falling backward from the top of the deck into the pool below.

A twenty-five-foot green screen wall was constructed behind the ship to allow the VFX team to extend the scope of the scene—adding the expanse of a harbor filled with ships.

OPPOSITE: With barrels, debris, and a rowboat in the pool below the ship, the set is prepared for the scene where the guards come to Charlotte's rescue.

The broken masts on the ship's deck were added with matte painting.

The shots of the prison ship in the harbor required 3-D water, in some cases combined with real water. One of the 3-D artists, who specialized in fluid simulation, did the work. The challenge with 3-D water is getting it to interact with other elements correctly. For instance, floating barrels and ships need to move with the water.

The existing deck and stern of the ship were extended digitally with a combination of 3-D and 2-D effects to create the full ship. The VFX team used still photographs of the existing set and placed them onto the 3-D ship model that they designed.

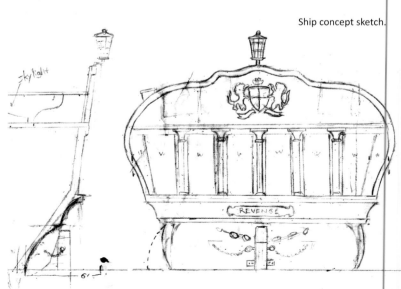

Ship concept sketch.

The original 3-D ship model.

The fully developed prison ship sits in the harbor among the other
unfinished 3-D models.

CARRIAGE

RIGHT: The carriage in its prison coach form.

"The carriage was a really exciting piece to see come together," Nick recalls. With humble beginnings as a retired wedding buggy purchased on Craigslist, it came with a pop-up top and vinyl sides that were anything but period. But it had some very desirable aspects. The wheel structure was appropriate for the period, with the wheels in the front being much smaller than the ones in the back. "Many of the carriages we looked at did not have this feature," Nick says. "We thought about building the carriage on a wagon bed because they're much easier to find, but their wheels are all the same size, and that is a dead giveaway that it's not a carriage." The carriage's base was well built and solid. After the team had stripped off the vinyl top and other accessories, such as taillights and handles, they built a 1770s carriage frame right on the buggy's base.

Over the course of the film, this carriage appears as three different coaches. "We had the East India Company carriage which had gold trim, the prison carriage which was black with barred windows and rivets, and the New York smuggler's carriage which was maroon and gold," says Nick. "For many of the shots we kept one side of the carriage painted as the East India Company coach and the other as the prison carriage. But we switched the paint schemes many times. We would pop off all the rivets and repaint the whole thing. Then the next week we would need it to be the prison carriage, so we would redo it all again."

BELOW (LEFT TO RIGHT): A 2x4 frame is added to the wedding buggy. Particleboard and foam complete the carriage exterior. The DP guides the camera and crane as the carriage comes to a stop. A stunt carriage was built for the explosion.

The smuggler's carriage. Although it is not visible in this photo, the other side of the carriage is painted to be the East India Company carriage.

Nathan Burns
PROPS

"The property master has to supervise and organize the construction and distribution of the props. I oversee them all the way from sketching them to getting them in the actors' hands in the scene."

A great fit for the role, Nathan Burns is studying engineering and loves drawing and model building. Age sixteen at the time of production, he had a team of guys working for him on props. The job had a lot of responsibility. "One of the most stressful parts was keeping things organized. We had to keep track of the hundreds of props, always knowing exactly where they were so that they would be available when we needed them."

Creating the right look for the props was a fun challenge. "With the carriage bomb, we were trying to figure out what sort of explosive charge to use. Originally we were going for the classic dynamite stick style, but dynamite wasn't invented until the 1900s. So we went with some light gunpowder charges in glass jars. We also used piano gears to achieve a mechanical, steampunk effect.

"The prop weapons needed to reflect the varied cultures that they represented. We had the Indian sword for Basil as well as the tiger claw. The colonials had clubs and guns, and for the British forces we had muskets. Will's East India Company sniper rifle was a blend of British and Indian. The curved stock and the ivory elephant represent the Indian influence, yet the barrel and lock were made in the English style."

TOP: Five colonial muskets were handcrafted by Indian guildsmen for the film.

LEFT: The burning carriage bomb was created by a combination of sparks from a fuse and flickering light from a lightbulb on a dimmer switch.

TO RENT.
A three story HOUSE,

On the main street in this City, a few doors from the Courthouse. This House is well calculated to accommodate a genteel family, and is in complete repair. The terms may be known by applying to

John Beale.

Richmond, April 24, 1802.

LEFT: The front of the Henry Ford Museum is an exact replica of Independence Hall in Philadelphia. Here the crew works in the drizzly weather outside the museum.

ABOVE: The historic face of Independence Hall is commemorated on coins and stamps.

OPPOSITE: Both cameras focus on the slate before filming a shot. The digital timer and the clapper help to precisely align the footage with the audio.

INDEPENDENCE HALL

"We knew that we could never replicate Independence Hall, but we needed this location for the end of the movie. We also knew that there was no way we could logistically move the entire crew out to Philadelphia," Nick says. "Aaron and I were brainstorming about how to work around these issues with our locations manager Brian Ervin when Brian mentioned that we could look into using the Henry Ford Museum for the set. We were shocked to discover that there was a copy of Independence Hall right here in Michigan!"

Few people know that when Henry Ford built his museum in Dearborn, Michigan, he built the front as an exact replica of Philadelphia's Independence Hall—even down to the building's flaws. This location was only sixty minutes from *Beyond the Mask's* production lot, well within reach for the team. The interior entrance was also historically accurate, providing a complete set for Independence Hall.

GENERATOR ROOM

OPPOSITE: (TOP) Original concepts showed the underwater hideout constructed beneath a ship sitting in Philadelphia Harbor.
(BOTTOM LEFT) Concept sketch of Kemp's underwater laboratory.
(BOTTOM RIGHT) The series of Leyden jars with flickering lightbulbs and dry ice added for effect.

Kemp's generator room, the film's final set, was the largest and most complex set in *Beyond the Mask*. "Early on in the project, we were looking for a place to have our villain's secret generator lab," recalls Nick. "I had drawn some Jules Verne–flavored concept art of an underwater laboratory which was accessed by an elevator shaft running down from the hold of a ship. This was fun, but we wanted something less fantastical and based more soundly in the history of Philadelphia. That was when we stumbled upon Windmill Island." Standing in the Delaware River, the island was formed around the hull of a sunken vessel. So they wrote into the script the concept that Kemp had built the generator beneath Windmill Island, pumping out the water from the ship and sealing it off to use as a laboratory.

Working from this premise, Nick decided to construct the set inside an old Gothic-roofed barn on the production lot. The barn was nothing special from the outside, with its peeling paint and missing shingles—in fact, the landlord was intending to tear it down. It was ideal for this set, however, and the inside looked for all the world like an upside-down ship's hull. The walls and ceiling were made entirely of dark wooden planks. "We could not have asked for a better location," Nick says. "This place was incredible!"

The first prop built for this set was the electrostatic generator wheel. This set piece was a replica of Franklin's electrostatic generator, only this one was much larger, reaching over twelve feet in height. "There was no way we could have made the wheel out of real wood," Nick says. "It would have been far too heavy and cumbersome to work with. So we went with our old friend Styrofoam."

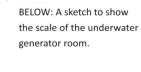

BELOW: A sketch to show the scale of the underwater generator room.

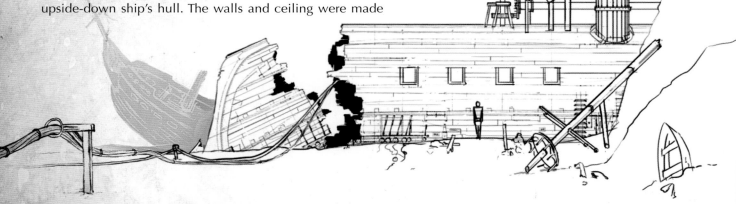

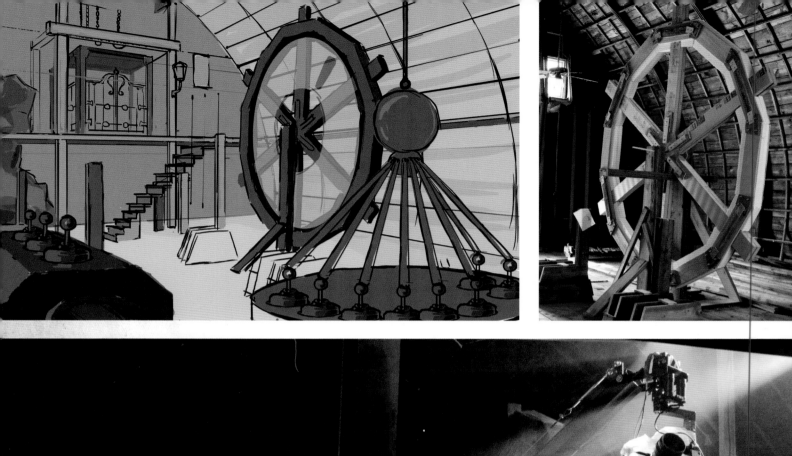

Once the frame was constructed, the team spread thin-set mortar over the entire piece, carving wood grain into it before it dried. Over six washes of paint were then applied to give it a realistic wood look. The piece was finished when an engineer attached gears to the side and made the wheel spin to life. The wheel was one of many props that the team built in the generator room. The barn was empty when they started, but in one month they filled it with catwalks, Leyden jars, platforms, control panels, and wires linking everything together. This was a complete 360-degree set that could be filmed from any angle. Once the underwater lighting was in place, the run-down barn was completely transformed. "It totally blew me away," Nick recalls. "I felt like I was in a different place."

OPPOSITE: (TOP LEFT) Concept art of the generator room's layout. (TOP RIGHT) The electrostatic wheel in its initial stages of construction, with the pink foam still clearly visible. (BOTTOM) The finished wheel stood twelve feet high and was rotated by belts running down to the barn's basement.

TOP: The condemned barn houses the underwater lab.

MIDDLE: Blue light through the windows added to the underwater atmosphere with the contrast of warm yellow representing firelight.

BOTTOM: The doctor's control panel was constructed using random parts, giving it a steampunk look. A set of old piano hammers was even incorporated.

FOLLOWING PAGE: A still from the generator room.

Windmill_Tower

*T*he twenty-foot-tall base of the windmill was constructed on the production property in Michigan, but the rest of the structure, including the tower and blades, and the explosion were all computer generated. The windmill stands nearly ninety feet tall in the film, but creating the explosion was far more complicated than simply building the machine.

Each shot had to be aligned to tell the same story. The team laid out the shots with what they called a "battle board" (pictured at right). This allowed them to see the progression from beginning to end. Luke, the visual effects coordinator, explains the challenge: "It was important to know where the fire should be at what point, and where the windmill should fall and when. We had to figure out how the fire would move up the tower and explode the top and dislodge the blades. We had to time it so the windmll blade would enter the water at the correct time."

LEFT: An untextured draft of the 3-D windmill.

TOP: The camera was located at the end of the dock to film this tight shot of Will and Charlotte running from the elevator shaft's flames.

ABOVE: The camera was then moved across the lake and the explosion was filmed again with no actors. Next, Kara and Andrew were filmed diving into the lake from the same angle and the shots were composited together.

Nick Burns
DESIGN

"The production designer is responsible for the look and feel of the film," says Nick Burns. "This basically covers everything that you see: wardrobe, sets, props, hair, makeup, effects. Although I'm not directly in charge of each department, it is my job to interface between them and the director, making sure that his artistic vision for the film gets to the screen.

"Months before preproduction began, I started working with Chad to develop a look for each character and the different environments our movie was going to take place in. We had to define what *Beyond the Mask's* version of the East India Company was going to look like, what our versions of England and Philly were going to feel like, what aspect of history *Beyond the Mask* was going to highlight, how to incorporate the different technology from the time, and so forth. I spent weeks sketching—working to get our ideas on paper.

"Once preproduction hit, I was in charge of coordinating the construction of the sets, props, and costumes. Decisions had to be made as to which sets could be replaced with green screen and which sets had to be built. The challenge was to give the film a large-scale period feeling on a limited budget and with limited time. As a rule, we found that the accepted methods for constructing sets and props were too expensive, so it often came down to research and ingenuity as we developed our own way of achieving the same effects within our budget. Once filming start- ed, a lot of time was spent repurposing sets. This meant staying up all night to change a set from a previous scene into a completely new set for an upcoming scene. One of the classic transformations was the interior of Franklin's shop turning into the pub. This was a pretty significant transformation. My best memories are all the late nights and strenuous work as a team.

"The art team was small, but each person had a different realm of experience that he brought into the project. It was really cool to see their different areas of expertise come into play as we figured out where to position them on the team and which different set or prop projects to assign them. They were all great people, and I really enjoyed working with them. They had great attitudes, were hardworking, and were always willing to go the extra mile. That was the secret that allowed us to accomplish so much as a team."

Nick discusses the shot's framing with Chad.

A **COLONIAL CAST**

Photo by David Heisler   Photo by Christianne Taylor

ABOVE LEFT: Andrew Cheney.   ABOVE RIGHT: Kara Killmer.

Candidates submit their professional acting headshots to the casting director for review in the audition process. A good headshot can make all the difference, since the casting director decides who to call in for auditions based on the initial review of these photos.

Beverly Holloway
CASTING DIRECTOR

"The casting director is tasked with taking the director's vision for the characters and then searching the pools of talent to find the available options and bring them to the table ultimately for the director and producer to choose from," outlines Beverly Holloway, the Los Angeles casting director.

"I had been in a different field earlier [in my career] and was doing management and interior design in a theater . . . I thought that a skill set for the film world was something that I might be suited for. I'm kind of a mix of creative and business, which I think most casting directors are. I got an opportunity to intern on one of [my friend's] projects. That's really where I started. I worked in production [as well] but ultimately, casting was the area that I was most passionate about and I think most suited for, so I eventually focused all my effort in the area of casting."

For Beverly, one of the most challenging elements of the job on *Beyond the Mask* was the historical nature of the film. "You'd be surprised how many people would come into the audi-

tion setting, people who were otherwise great actors—very talented people—who didn't feel right for this story, because they just didn't fit this era. There's just a relaxed quality or a very contemporary feel to how someone comes across. It wouldn't matter if you put them in costume and surrounded them with period props and sets—they would feel out of place." Appropriate speech patterns were also a concern. "We had the British accent for the scenes that were taking place in England and also Indian because of the story line and then of course the Americans. But they were new Americans [who] hadn't lost all of their English ancestry. They sounded different from those in the English settings. So there were a lot of those different kinds of nuances that made it both unique and challenging on that front because you obviously don't want to ignore those things. You want that part of the character to be as strong as possible so that it doesn't become distracting in the story as people are watching it. That was probably the most unique characteristic in the process."

ABOVE: A page from the William Reynolds casting sides. Actors memorize their character's sides, or an excerpt from the script, and prepare to present the scene to the casting director during their auditions.

John Kirby
ACTING COACH

"I delve into the script to build these characters and bring to life their words. I like to find a way to make it very personal," acting coach John Kirby says. John has worked as an acting coach for over thirty years and has coached on many well-known films including *The Count of Monte Cristo, Peter Pan,* and *The Chronicles of Narnia: The Lion the Witch and the Wardrobe.* In his early twenties, he opened the John Kirby Studio in Los Angeles, where he continues to teach when not on location. Among his stable of actors is his long-time client Jim Caviezel, whom he has coached since he was twenty-two. John also directed Thomas Nelson's audio Bible, *The Word of Promise: Next Generation,* starring Sean Astin, which won an Audie for best nonfiction inspirational book of 2011.

Beyond the Mask first came to his notice while he was preparing his private clients to read for Beverly Holloway, the project's LA casting director, as well as his student Kara Killmer, whom he had introduced to Bev on a previous project. "I was reading the script and I flipped over it," remembers John. "I thought, 'What a remarkable movie!' The story was so wonderful, and the message was strong and beautifully executed. I was glad to see that finally a script in the Christian market was able to tell the message without ever feeling trite or cliché or heavy-handed. I was just knocked out by it. This is a great story with so much texture and has so many tremendous characters to explore. It was beautiful.

"Then the phone rang one day. It was Bev, and she said, 'They want you to coach on the project.' I said, 'This is incredible! I hope it works out because I really want to be a part of this project,' and I don't say that very often. So they worked it all out and sent Andrew and Kara [the actors playing William Reynolds and Charlotte Holloway] to me.

"Kara is a student of mine, and we have worked together for over two years. We have a rare creative relationship, and she trusts me. She never disagrees, never argues. She says, 'Okay, that's what you see, I'm going to dig in, and I'm going to find that,' and sure enough she gets in front of the camera and it is all there.

"Andrew and I had met briefly once, but I really didn't know him even though, ironically, we live on the same road in Studio City. Andrew is a special talent and a great human being. I think we are going to see such remarkable things for his future in the industry.

"The camaraderie shared between me, Kara, and Andrew was pretty special and created such a sense of trust. We enjoy each other, we get the work done. We prepare before we go to set, we prepare when we get off set, and we just roll with it all. I love working personally with the actors because you start to find where certain things begin for them, or what if and how their imaginations open up, and as you talk to each individual you start to see what parts of them they can bring into these characters. Kara and Andrew are such willing actors, so willing to explore, and so open to

OPPOSITE: John waits with Andrew and Kara for a rehearsal at Scripps Mansion. John was with the talent in all their spare moments.

finding those parts which are sometimes very hard to find, and willing to live in that vulnerability. Kara finds this bravery that Charlotte takes on, and the length she goes to to save Will is so remarkable. And Andrew has such a heart as a human being that when we come to these scenes where he is so torn, and so confused, and wants so desperately to change and please Charlotte, it just breaks your heart. And the chemistry that Kara and Andrew share on the screen is spectacular. It has really been a tremendous thing to watch. It is just so beautiful.

"I truly am so grateful and blessed to have worked with Chad and Aaron and all the Burns family who, aside from their extraordinary gifts of so many talents, bring such love and grace to moviemaking. I will miss them all dearly when the film is over."

LEFT: John, Andrew, and Kara share stories about where they grew up on their first visit to set.

OPPOSITE: The costume designers worked diligently to give every outfit an authentic feel for the sake of the actors as well as the cameras. The wool for Kara's dress (pictured here) was purchased from a historic mill.

Andrew Cheney
WILLIAM REYNOLDS

*C*ontrary to the stereotype of a Hollywood star, Andrew Cheney does not live for the applause of a crowd. He is a man of character whose humility makes him a pleasure to meet. "Andrew made the effort to memorize and use everyone's name, and that meant a lot to us," says one of the grips. Andrew began his career in the business world after receiving his degree from Cedarville University but more recently relocated to Los Angeles to pursue acting. "We almost missed getting to work with Andrew," producer Aaron Burns says. "We had already gone through all twelve hundred of our LA auditions for the part, and we had our choices pretty well narrowed down. We had even closed out the audition process and moved on to chemistry reads before Andrew was brought to our attention. We asked him in for an audition, and we knew we had found William Reynolds." A gifted actor, Cheney brought to life the character of William Reynolds and powerfully portrayed his journey toward redemption. Meet Andrew here in an interview he did for *Beyond the Mask*.

BTM: What did you do to prepare for your role as Will?

Cheney: With any character that I'm planning to play, I'm always searching to understand more specifically who that character is, what that character wants, and what obstacles might stand in the way. This, of course, leads to exploration of the relationships, circumstances, time, and place that the character finds himself in. When it came to preparing to play Will, I wanted to understand him as specifically as the script could allow. So I buried myself in the script in the weeks and days prior to shooting as well as amidst shooting to discover as much about Will as I could. And for areas (such as parents, childhood, etc.) where the script left you guessing, I would create a backstory—additional details regarding a family, home life, social status, faith background, schooling etc. to allow for more specific choices throughout my performance.

Practically, there were the time period and action sequences to consider. So I spent some time working with a dialect coach (Joy Ellison—who was incredible!) and intensified my workouts and strength training to make sure I was ready for the choreography and stunt work. I do have to confess though that, as is true for a lot of us dudes, I'm still a little boy at heart. So the idea of getting to play an eighteenth-century crime-fighting vigilante assassin is something I feel like I've been preparing for . . . since I was ten.

I also had the wonderful privilege of having John Kirby by my side guiding me through a lot of this process as well. John is just an incredible guy. His wisdom, experience, counsel, and dedication were incredibly helpful in my preparation.

BTM: How do you relate to Will's spiritual journey?

Cheney: Will's journey was defined by the need to redeem his name . . . to create a new identity that was honorable enough to be loved. And in efforts to achieve this end, he found himself hiding. I can definitely relate to hiding. I believe we all wrestle with hiding behind false identities. We may not be literally changing our name, or disguising our face, but so often we find ourselves searching for worth in the ways our culture has defined for us . . . in our

ABOVE: This church steeple set was constructed inside a pole barn located on the studio property.

RIGHT: Reynolds and his men were part of the EIC's ruthless rule in India. The India set where Will's flashbacks were shot was created from the remains of the hill fort built for the film *Pendragon*.

BELOW: Concept art for Reynolds's EIC assassin gear.

EIC ASSASSIN

achievement, our wealth, in our status, or in our personal holiness. Though I've not found myself fighting crime in my off-hours just yet, I have had to come face-to-face with the question of where do I find worth, my significance. And it's a question we're all faced with at many points throughout our lives. And it's an easy one to shove aside . . . but we all reach that point where we can't ignore it anymore.

BTM: *Could you share a bit of your personal faith journey?*
Cheney: Growing up in the home of a pastor, I came to faith in Christ at an early age. I was blessed to be raised by parents who cherish the truth of the gospel, cherish each other, and have always been supportive of my pursuits and my faith. That said, I still had to make my faith something that I was going to pursue, not just something I did because my parents told me it was good. That decision came in high school for me. And as I've encountered life's blessings and

challenges, trials and tribulations since then, I'm continually challenged to answer more deeply and more completely the questions—Who am I? Where do I find my significance? What do I hold ultimate? Where does my strength come from? My hope and prayer is that, as my faith is continually tried and tested, I will continually be able to say with boldness, my strength is in Him.

BTM: *Briefly state the message of* Beyond the Mask.
Cheney: At its core, *Beyond the Mask* is a film all about identity. Through Will's journey and Charlotte's urgings, we are forced to ask of ourselves, "Where do I find my hope, my significance, my worth?"

BTM: *What aspect of the movie's spiritual theme do you think is important for young people?*
Cheney: We live in an age where identity seems threatened and confused by culture more than ever before. The voices of the modern world glorify feelings . . . truth is relative . . . it's what you feel. Couple that with pop culture's relentless proclamation that fame, fortune, success, and a whole lot of sexy will bring you all the happiness in the world, and you've got a mountain of influence to deal with. I think this creates a very difficult environment for kids to truly ground themselves in truth . . . and really blurs their source of significance and worth. I know at times it has for me. My hope is that Will's journey and Charlotte's firm grounding really speak to the power of sifting through the voices of culture, discerning truth, and hearing the call of the gospel to ground our identity firmly in Christ.

ABOVE: Chad and Andrew rehearse the moment when Will confronts Kemp at the masquerade.

Traditional 1700s vicar garb.

Reynolds runs from Kemp's men after being discovered in Addlesbury.

Even as he takes refuge in the quiet English countryside,
Will cannot escape the vivid flashbacks from India.

BTM: What makes Chad's directing style unique?

Cheney: The answer to that question comes in the form of a compliment to his character. As Chad is a truly humble and generous man, he is uniquely humble and generous as a director. When it came to collaborating on character choices, dialogue, or blocking, Chad had a humility in the way he received input and suggestions all while holding true to the original vision. Chad was also very giving throughout the shoot. Not only was he generous with his feedback, but he made time with each of us a priority. He made it a point to spend time not only discussing the scenes and story, but really prioritized creating a relationship with us as people, not just actors on his set. This went a long way for me . . . not only did his leadership create a safe environment in which to work and explore, but it made for a really enjoyable life on set.

BTM: What is Kara's personality like off camera?

Cheney: Well, well, well . . . this is a fun one. In a single word . . . wait, no, I need at least three . . . I would describe Kara's personality as adventurous, empathetic, and goofy. In a given day with Kara, I would find myself bouncing from stories about her geological exploration of the Grand Canyon to culinary exploration of octopus to spot-on, performance-grade impressions of John Kirby, Chad Burns, her college roommate, or any Disney character you can name (seriously, she's incredible). If it was a particularly special day, I might be so privileged as to hear Kara play one of her songs she's composed on the piano, or perform a rap she's written about William Reynolds's pursuit of Charlotte (keep your eyes out for the soundtrack!), or watch her freestyle a song about our AD, Chip Lake, in between takes. Kara seriously is one enormously gifted performer . . . her love for it is so innocent, childlike, and pure, and she is so wonderfully generous with it. Couple that with incredibly sincere warmth and the ability to speak her mind in the most charming of ways, and it made for a set life with Kara that was anything but boring. But she's not just an entertainer. Kara truly is a woman of great substance and complexity. If you ever had the chance to visit Kara's trailer, you'd see a glimpse into what a tender, creative, compassionate woman of faith she truly is. Kara has what I might call a "knack for nesting." So as early as the third week of shooting, Kara was quite comfortably settled in. Quotes, poems, sketches, paintings, and a multitude of

ABOVE: Kara and Andrew pause for a quick snapshot together before diving off the dock in their escape from the exploding windmill.

FAR RIGHT: Starting with this simple sleeveless coat, Will develops his highwayman disguise over the course of the film.

RIGHT: An early idea of the highwayman mask.

BELOW: Concept art depicting Reynolds's highwayman costume.

John and Andrew receive
instructions from the stuntman
before their sword fight.

Scripture covered her trailer walls. It was a window into what drives her, and it was beautiful. Kara is such a wonderful combination of whimsy and intellect, and she truly is blessed with such a compassionate, pure, and faithful heart. Okay, okay, so maybe even three words don't do her justice.

BTM: What was it like acting across from JRD?

Cheney: Working with John Rhys-Davies really was a tremendous privilege. I've been a fan of John's work since I was a child, so to get to act across from him truly was an honor. John brought so many uniquely personal and dynamic nuances to the character of Charles Kemp, and he was constantly uplifting those across from him. With that perfectly pitched voice and the kind of classic charm only he can deliver, he would frequently end a take with a big smile and a self-deprecating, "You were best." John always brought such a cheerful, charming presence to set and was extremely generous. Given John's vast amount of experience with stunt work and fight choreography, I also had an incredible time hearing story after story recounting his harrowing adventures on sets around the world. It was an honor, and I'd love to work with him again someday.

BELOW AND RIGHT: Since the backstory of *Beyond the Mask* takes place in East India, the Indian culture influenced many costume designs throughout the film, especially Will's signature coat.

ABOVE: Andrew makes friends with everyone on set. Here he plays with Carlee Zale, the little girl whom the highwayman rescues from the burning building.

OPPOSITE: (TOP LEFT) The finishing touch on Will's highwayman costume is the engagement ring that he desperately wants to present to Charlotte. (BOTTOM LEFT) Reynolds discovers gunpowder underneath Independence Hall. (RIGHT) Multiple long days of rehearsal took place with the cast in preparation for filming the final scene in the generator room.

CHARLOTTE HOLLOWAY

C asting for the role of Charlotte Holloway was a difficult task. Over sixteen hundred actresses applied for the part. Ironically, having only received the script late the night before, Kara Killmer was the last actress to audition for the role. Chad and Aaron had flown out to California for the casting process and were present at the audition. Watching her performance, they were impressed right away. "When Kara left the audition room, we looked at each other, and we knew we had found our star," says Chad.

Kara is a very gifted actress and has done extensive work on the stage as well as for television and film. On her first day of shooting, she gave fans a brief update. "This is Kara Killmer, and I'm playing Charlotte Holloway. We've just finished shooting, and it's been a really good day. I was very nervous and excited at the beginning of the day, but you know, it's all under the blanket of 'God's in control,' so that always lifts the burden. I can't wait until tomorrow. And even though I'm in so many layers, I still love my costume." She added with a smile: "I have always wanted to be in a period piece, and I am so excited to be going on this grand adventure!"

Kara's personality brings enthusiasm to every aspect of life. Fun to be around, she is always interacting positively with those around her. "There's so much strength to her, so much independence, yet this gentle femininity as well," Andrew Cheney describes her. "She has a real youthful energy." She also loves to entertain. As Chad puts it, "Kara is from the class of actors who love performing. If they're telling a story and all of a sudden the whole room goes hushed to hear what they're saying, they don't miss a beat. They don't get nervous. They relish that moment. Kara has this characteristic, and she leverages it well.

What that means is that although she prepares very well, she's flexible when she comes to set. She really has a charming personality. She seems to enjoy herself and have fun with her work, and it reads on camera."

Because Kara shares a solid personal faith in Christ with this eighteenth-century girl, the message of the film was deeply meaningful to her on a personal level. Kara explains her summary of the film's message: "This movie attempts to address the question: what is it that makes you who you are? What we find in the film is that it's really Christ and our relationship with the Lord that defines us and gives us a sense of strength and centeredness . . . We parade around with the self-burden of many masks, but part of the joy of salvation in Jesus Christ is to put on the ultimate mask of adopted son or daughter and put off the wretched façades of this dark world."

Sharing about her connection with the role, Kara says, "Ever since I read the script, the character Charlotte has caught my imagination. Throughout the film she shows herself to have a beautiful blend of wisdom and femininity, replicating Matthew chapter 6 perfectly, as 'wise as a serpent, but as gentle as a dove.'" In the film's story, Charlotte is the one who shows Will what it looks like to be secure in one's identity. She knows who she is in Christ, yet she is still exploring how her Christ-centeredness works out in the world. When faced with great difficulty, she responds with solid faith. "Charlotte has a strong sense that she cannot go out and face any of these circumstances without relying on her faith. In the film, you see the male figures in Charlotte's life shift around a lot. In the beginning of the film, her father has passed away. She doesn't have a father. She has no brothers. She is an only child, so she's relying heavily on her uncle's influence to be the man in her life, and then William comes along as Stephen Walters. For Charlotte this may be the beginning of having a close man in her life. [But] I think what's great about Charlotte is that she's . . . always looking to God to be the authority in her life, which is a good example for all of us girls, because it's so easy for us to get wrapped up in leaning on whatever man is around."

Although the script provided some details about Charlotte, Kara greatly expanded on them to create a believable character with many layers of depth. She worked very diligently and imaginatively to develop her character, and she would frequently elaborate on the rest of Charlotte's story, such as her and Basil's plan to get married, take over the East India Company, and move to India to raise a dozen children. Well, maybe she wasn't serious about that one . . .

Our on-location acting coach, John Kirby, was Kara's personal coach, so their existing relationship made it easy for them to work

TOP: John Kirby works with Kara to bring the character of Charlotte Holloway to life.

BOTTOM: The recovery room set was created in the corner of a large hallway in Scripps Mansion.

CHARLOTTE HOLLOWAY - **WALKING DRESS**

CHARLOTTE HOLLOWAY - **BALL GOWN**

Marilyn Burns
WARDROBE DESIGNER

*B*eginning work months before production starts, the wardrobe designer takes the clothing in the film from concept to reality—she tells the story through the costumes. Marilyn learned to sew at a young age and has designed costumes for both film and stage productions. A very driven person, she is very creative and gifted at improvising. Marilyn is also a great leader and headed up a team of ten to thirty wardrobe personnel over the months of preproduction and production. The team transformed her house into both a workshop and a dormitory.

Marilyn had to design within the distinctive constraints of colonial fashions. "One of the interesting elements in this particular time period is the overwhelming number of buttons on colonial clothes. They didn't have zippers, so they pretty much buttoned everything. Every shirt has buttons. Every waistcoat has buttons. A single pair of britches requires seventeen buttons, and a coat could require anywhere from thirty to forty, depending on how decorative it is. Altogether, we bought or made several thousand buttons for the costumes.

"We also worked really hard to get the right materials for the period—real wool and linen, and real silk taffeta, as opposed to the polyester or synthetics that we use today. These natural fiber materials wear very differently than synthetics, and you can tell the difference on

...amera. We ordered a lot of our wool from an heir-loom mill that has been around since before the Civil War. A lot of the silks we ordered from overseas, and we even ordered some fabric from India.

"We designed our underpinnings to look authentic, but we had to be creative with the materials we used because of the expense. Women's stays and pocket hoops would have been made of either metal or bone, but we used pieces of plastic zip ties for the stays and miniature PVC pipes for the hoops, which was significantly cheaper than metal.

"Some interesting challenges came up when the actors had to deal with things like horseback riding or even being in a saltwater pool. We had to really think ahead about the kinds of materials we were going to use and how the actors needed to move and how the materials would react."

together. "I love John Kirby. I have a long history with John. He's been there since the beginning of my journey in Hollywood, so it was a big, big treat to get to have my mentor here with me on my first film," Kara says. "His ability to articulate the humanity of a character is so rare, and it's so specific to him . . . John is very Christlike in his critiquing of actors' work. He never tears someone down to get a point across. He has a very positive and brilliant technique as a coach, and I'm so grateful for him. I wouldn't have wanted anyone else to accompany me on this journey." Kara and John worked together to interpret the story. "My script is very colorful; it's all tabbed up and highlighted, and there are notes everywhere with really tiny writing that I can't even read," Kara relates.

Each night after shooting, Kara, Andrew, and John would go back to the hotel and spend several hours preparing for their upcoming scenes. The rest of her method for getting into character was to adopt Charlotte's accent and wardrobe. "Putting on the costume and picking up the dialect will get you 90 percent into character. It changes your posture and your speech, and the whole façade will take it from there."

But how similar are Kara Killmer and Charlotte Holloway to each other? "I feel very at home in Charlotte's shoes. I think we care about the same things. I think we have the same apprehension about love, and we have the same attachment to our faith and our family. And I think we both want to believe the best about the people who are around us, so it's easy for me to go in and out of being her." But Kara and Charlotte's

ABOVE: John Rhys-Davies and Kara glance into a mirror in conversation.

personalities diverge when it comes to British manners. "[Charlotte is] much more of a lady than I am. I'm quite sassy, and she's so put together, but at the end [of the film] she gets a little rough and tough. She's ready to break out from her corseted life and embrace the adventure. But if it were me, I would just be hair waving and running around all the time on prison ships and jumping off the end of them and climbing trees. I would be a terrible example of a lady in 1775," Kara explains with a twinkle in her eye.

Wardrobe was a big part of her day, and Kara appreciated the sophistication of Charlotte's gowns. Thanks to Marilyn, the costume designer, many intricate details were woven into her wardrobe. Her clothes were historically accurate—even the undergarments. Although Kara enjoyed wearing colonial costumes for a few weeks, she expressed her relief that modern fashion does not require the presence of a corset. While shooting the scene where Charlotte attends church, she described the effects of her silk taffeta gown: "I feel very elegant. I feel like a princess. Certainly if I don't catch Will with this dress, there's no hope at all."

Because so much of the film occurs after dark, there were lots of night shoots. Turning nocturnal is exhausting for anyone, because you inevitably get less sleep. "You can't really tell when you should be awake or when you should be asleep based on when the sun is out. It's all about to what degree you feel like you've been hit by a truck. If you feel like you've gotten to the 'I've been hit by a freight train' stage, that's when you know you're supposed to go to sleep and that you've been doing too many night shoots." For Kara, as well as much of the crew, the solution was caffeine, and hot coffee was a constant presence on set. Kara claimed to have drunk more coffee on production than the combination of all previous cups in her life and cited it as her favorite snack on a night shoot. What did Kara's typical schedule on set look like? "Coffee. Makeup. Hair. Costume. Coffee. Stand on a mark and say some lines. Cut. Stay on the same mark and say the same lines again while the camera is at a different angle. Repeat. Coffee. Repeat. Coffee. Lunch . . . in a corset. Coffee. Act. Act. Act. Coffee. De-corset. Prep scenes for next day. Sleep."

While filming the movie's climax, Kara was tied to the base of the electrostatic generator every day for a whole week. Needless to say, she was quite excited to finish that scene and rejoiced in the absence of her rope bonds. Kara was always finding opportunities to have fun on set and took advantage of the time between takes to make up songs or do some freestyle "colonial" tap dancing. One day when there was a replica pistol on set, she picked it up with a sly grin and said with a wink at the camera, "[Here's a] sequel for you."

Kara had a great working relationship with the crew, and they enjoyed her vibrant presence on set. Although she maintained a professional attitude, she was happy to interact with the crew and cared about them on a personal level. "What I loved about working with this crew was its genuine harmony. There wasn't an ego in sight. Every person was fully committed to the vision of the movie and became a close family very quickly," Kara says. The crew was

ABOVE: Even at 3 a.m. on freezing night shoots, Kara's cheerful spirit kept the crew smiling.

ABOVE: On the last day of principal photography, the crew filmed the escape from the prison ship in an indoor saltwater pool.

OPPOSITE: Will and Charlotte's escape from the generator room was filmed in several different locations. (TOP RIGHT) The first part was filmed inside the original set. (BOTTOM) Next, grabbing the rope was filmed inside the production lot pole barn. (TOP LEFT) Then the escape onto the dock was filmed at a separate outdoor location.

excited about the opportunity to work on a film that brought glory to God, and the unity and love they expressed impacted Kara. She describes the spirit of the crew as "what God intends the entire Christian community to be." Never above others, Kara has a humble spirit, and she invested in the individual crew members, building friendships with them. Peter Burns, a member of the assistant directing team, who is also involved in politics, was one example. All in fun, Kara declared him a presidential candidate with herself as his personal campaign manager. For the remaining weeks of the shoot this was a running joke, and Kara could be heard calling out spontaneously, "Peter Burns for president!"

Chad and Kara had a lot of respect for each other, and their collaboration was very profitable. "What is great about working with Chad as a director is that he is very receptive. In general, most directors seem to have an idea in their mind and they're closed to any input. But Chad is very flexible with our vision as actors, which is uncommon, and it feels very safe for us. It's so nice to have a director who is willing to listen and is willing to explore with you."

Kara and Andrew also enjoyed working together. They had never met before the film project, but the two of them worked well together as hero and heroine. When asked about working with Kara, Andrew says: "What a gift. There was an instant connection with Kara. She brings a lot to who Charlotte is, and it works really well. There's really been a big trust that we've developed. It's really a privilege when you can establish that so firmly, because it's not always the case, and so to have that connection with her has been a real pleasure." And Kara says of Andrew in turn, "It is very rare to have someone that you have to spend so much time with, that you have to have a romantic role with as well, who is so kind. Andrew is very considerate. He's very attentive, and he works so hard. He's been so good about taking care of me as a scene partner and a friend."

It's clear from her performance that Kara Killmer was the perfect one to bring the character of Charlotte Holloway to life on screen, and she loved the part. "It's both strange and wonderful acting for the camera. On one hand you feel like you are baring your soul in front of an intrusive black box. On the other hand, as an actor, it feels like home. The joy of telling and capturing a great story is extremely rewarding . . . especially one as exciting as this!"

On her last day of shooting, the crew applauded as Kara finished her final scene. But leaving Charlotte's world was a bittersweet moment for Kara. Full of emotion, she said farewell. "We just finished my last shot, and I am wrapped, so I get to go home, and I have to say good-bye to the character of Charlotte Holloway. Everyone's been so wonderful, I couldn't ask for a better film to be the first film that I get to work on. And I'm going to miss everybody so much, it's just been such a caring environment and such a good story to tell, which is the best any actor can ask for is to just tell a really good story. So thank you for giving me the chance and letting me live out my biggest dreams for the first time."

OPPOSITE: Relaxing while the crew resets, Andrew and Kara were friends off-camera as well.

RIGHT: Kara brought a light-hearted smile to the set. Here she laughs with Chad and his wife, Angela.

John Rhys-Davies
CHARLES KEMP

*L*iving in front of the camera is an art that John Rhys-Davies has learned well. He approaches his acting with gusto and energy. A consummate performer, Rhys-Davies is always acting whether he is in front of the camera or not. He is a true showman.

John's can-do and go-getter attitude has taken him on a long and exciting journey. Over the years, he has played supporting roles in literally hundreds of feature films. He has worked with Steven Spielberg, George Lucas, and Peter Jackson. His truly amazing talent and hard work have allowed his career to intersect with all the greats in the industry. "John is a really big name, and having him on set was quite an honor," says director Chad Burns. Most beloved for his role in *Lord of the Rings*, John's enduring portrayal of Gimli has won him a place in the hearts of millions of fans around the country and the world.

"I love swash and buckle films. I love period pieces. I also like independent films that have their own strong values," John says of his time spent on *Beyond the Mask*, "and I love working with young directors who really know what they're doing."

The love of entertaining is built into John's personality, and he thrives on attention. On *Beyond the Mask*, every set that he walked onto was used to its full potential. John's sensitivity to his performances being captured was a benefit to the other cast members as well. In between takes, it was not unusual to see him showing less experienced actors where the lights were and telling them how they should stand to maximize the lighting

TOP: John Rhys-Davies is always ready with a witty line.
ABOVE: John and Kara rehearse before getting into costume for the masquerade ball.

in their situation. A master of his art, he worked organically to help the actors around him hit their marks.

John used a style of acting he called vamping. This meant that he only loosely followed the script, letting the emotions flow as the scene progressed. He wanted to do more than just recite lines; he wanted to be in the moment and worked to draw the other actors in with him. He had a strong desire to spar with the rest of the cast, which would lead to rich and interesting performances. John would often be heard telling the actor across from him to steal the scene from him. "I remember one time when he and Kara were doing a scene where they are arguing over the article that Charlotte has published after the night raid in America," Chad says with a smile. "They wound up going considerably off script. John was arguing with her about this situation, and Kara really rose to the occasion in a great way and did a good job of fighting him for the scene." Rhys-Davies loved this back-and-forth and enjoyed bringing the best out of the other actors.

John brought a lot of energy and intensity to every scene, but at the same time he was able to cultivate a lighthearted and almost playful environment on the set. "This was nice, because it is so easy during a heavy scene for the set to get a very melancholy feel," Kara says. "It was great to have John bring in his energy and put joy into motion by getting people excited and talking to everyone. He is very encouraging." John has a very generous personality and would often take time to reach out to the crew. He has the ability to make people feel welcome and at ease when he is around. "John Rhys-Davies is a very jovial man and would make a great Father Christmas character in any story," laughs Chad. This love of interacting with those around him encouraged the crew and made John a part of the team.

He thrived on weaving a good tale and could often be found surrounded by a group of people entertaining them with stories. Standing on set, you were likely to overhear him telling the camera crew the account of the time when the AC (assistant cameraman) fell off the boat while holding a massive camera or recounting the time when a wall collapsed on him in some exotic location.

John has a powerful presence on set. When the cameras are not rolling, he regails everyone around him with stories.

In addition to being an actor, John is also a scholar. He has a well-exercised mind and is well-rounded and well-read in the classics. "I had a great time talking about philosophy and religion with John," said Chad. "He has a great grasp on human nature, although I didn't necessarily agree with the conclusions he drew." John loves to write his own Greek ballads and was often sharing them with people on set between takes.

"I am deeply passionate about the preservation of a civilization that Christianity has brought into the world," says John, speaking on one of his favorite philosophy topics. "Those of us who believe in democracy, equality before the law, the equality of the sexes, the equality of races, the abolition of slavery, the right of free speech, the right of the individual conscience. If we do not defend these things to the best of our limited ability, we will lose them, and I think in Europe, we are well on the way to losing Europe as a western Christian civilization. This will be catastrophic for the world, and certainly for Europe."

ABOVE: Concept sketches of Kemp's wardrobe feature a blend of Britain and colonial India.

"It's very hard to find some redeeming qualities in Kemp. In fact, he is unredeemable, really," John explains when asked about his character. "He's very much like those Jane Austen characters who are genteel and kind and friendly at home but in fact are slave owners." John delved into his character, trying to understand what made Charles Kemp's actions justifiable to himself. His assessment was that Kemp was content with who he was. As Kemp himself says to Charlotte in *Beyond the Mask*, "Each of us must come to terms with our contradictions—I have." Summing up Kemp, John spontaneously quoted Shakespeare's *King Henry the Sixth*:

I have no brother, I am like no brother;
And this word 'love,' which graybeards call divine,
Be resident in men like one another
And not in me: I am myself alone.

THE ELEPHANT CANE

- A Gentleman's Secret -

"For Charles Kemp's cane, we needed something stylish that a gentleman would carry but also something with a darker purpose. The most important thing about the cane is the blade, which fits the character of Charles Kemp very well. He's very suave and very socially respected, but he wouldn't hesitate to stab you in the back. It's not the most powerful weapon, and certainly not as deadly as a gun, but it can be easily concealed for assassination. We wanted the blade to be able to come out very quickly, so that meant it had to be some sort of spring-loaded design. I came up with a very simple spring mechanism that would allow the blade to come out the end when the head of the cane was twisted. It extends up to seven inches and then locks in place. It can be retracted very quickly by twisting the head of the cane again."

Nathan Burns
Property Master

Adetokumboh M'Cormack
JOSHUA BRAND

"I remember reading the script thinking, 'This script is really, really good,'" Adetokumboh says about his introduction to *Beyond the Mask*. "I had never, ever seen a character like Joshua Brand in cinema. He wasn't the way that the media usually depicts African American people from that time period. I fell in love with this character. This man was articulate. He was evil and strong. I remember thinking, 'I've got to do this!' It's what I love doing most, and I just couldn't wait to get on set!" When asked how he related to the character of Joshua Brand, Ade laughs, saying, "I'm a geek! I love reading books and watching the news. I'm a complete nerd and the antithesis to what you see in the film."

Ade has an interesting life story, having been born in Sierra Leone to an American diplomat. He has since lived in Kenya, Nigeria, and Great Britain, and now resides in California. "It was a pleasure to work with Ade," director Chad Burns recalls. "He is a very gifted artist and has played in many films, including *Captain America: The Winter Soldier, Battle Los Angeles,* and *Blood Diamond*. He really leaned into the part and brought his enthusiasm to the set."

LEFT: Joshua Brand carries a concealed Indian dagger called a katar.

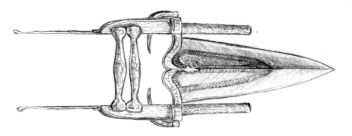

ABOVE: Brand fires a shot at Reynolds in the vicarage. A working flintlock pistol loaded with a blank was used in this scene.

LEFT: Concept sketch of the katar.

Samrat Chakrabarti
BASIL

Basil, Charles Kemp's right-hand man, was a fascinating character. Although the script never tells Basil's backstory, his Indian heritage implies that Kemp brought him back to England after his time in the Indies. Samrat Chakrabarti used the technique of method acting on *Beyond the Mask*. Deeply focused on his role as Basil, he stayed in character almost continually. It was a rare moment that a crew member would catch him being anything besides serious and grim, although there were definitely occasions when his hilarious personality would show through. He always seemed to enjoy giving the crew glimpses of how Basil would relate to the modern world and was observed to use Basil's tiger claw from time to time to type on his laptop or spear lettuce on lunch break.

LEFT: Samrat has played diverse roles and is know as a star in several romantic comedies.

ABOVE: Tiger claws are small, easily concealed weapons used in hand-to-hand combat.

Charlie Newhart
JEREMIAH FLACK

"*There* is only **one name** with the ***power*** to make you ***new***."

Ask any crew member about Charlie. He was a favorite on set. Angela Burns recalls, "We always really enjoyed having Charlie to set. He brought with him a contagious joy and spirit of gratefulness." Charlie's personal life experience strengthened his interpretation of his character. Having studied Nubian accents extensively for a previous role, he was able to use this skill to add depth to Jeremiah's character development, implying his origins on the African continent, which was a fun addition to the character. In the film, Jeremiah is shot, and many years ago, Charlie was actually shot while holding his infant son in his arms. This horrible experience was something Charlie used to draw from, and it gave him a much greater understanding and ability to relate to Jeremiah. But the most important aspect of Charlie's background is that he shares Jeremiah's faith, and upon committing his life to Jesus Christ, he changed his surname to "Newhart," a reference to Ezekiel 36:26: "I will give you a new heart and put a new spirit in you; I will remove from you your heart of stone and give you a heart of flesh." Charlie was very excited to be able to speak Jeremiah's line that means so much to him personally: "There is only one Name with the power to make you new."

RIGHT: Charlie believed in the message of *Beyond the Mask* and was eager to help bring the story to life.

MASQUERADE

PREVIOUS PAGE: Dancers line up for the Duke of Kent's Waltz.
BELOW: A string quartet serenades the party.
OPPOSITE: Charlotte and Will take their place at the head of a line of dancers.

The setting—a colonial masquerade ball. A myriad of deep colors and glittering golds dominate the party decor. Dozens of dancers strut in long rows, dressed in elaborately detailed costumes, all moving to the sweet melody of a string quartet perched on the stone patio. At the head of the line, the lead couple engage in serious conversation as they dip in and out of the other dancers' paths. Spotting the villain making a foul move at the far end of the crowd, the hero makes a swift exit.

The amount of sheer effort it takes to create one scene in a film is staggering to consider, yet the viewer only sees what is directly in front of the camera's lens. If the camera were to change direction momentarily and pan around to reveal what was behind it, what would be seen? How many people are at work that the audience never sees? What goes into making a scene? Consider for a moment a

bit of what each department put into just one scene from *Beyond the Mask*—the masquerade ball.

This scene is a critical turning point in the story. At the annual mayor's ball in New York, the film's hero, William Reynolds, is first shown to be the man he really is, and both he and Charlotte see their situation accurately. "It's a very powerful and important scene," says director Chad Burns. "The ball scene is where we go beyond the mask," where the audience discovers key truths about identity in Christ. Will is faced with the fact that he has been finding his identity in his own works. The façade is broken down, and he sees the situation clearly. He will never be able to do enough good to outweigh the evil he has done. Christ's work on his behalf is his only hope for justification.

The scale of the ball scene made it both extraordinarily difficult to produce and extremely satisfying to watch. The script called for rows of wealthy dancers in an extravagant setting, making Scripps Mansion ideal to host the party. This scene had the most extras, the most costumes, the most props, and the most of just about everything else. Except for the film's final set piece, the masquerade had more production value than any other scene in the film.

Although principal photography began in the heat of late summer, it was mid-October when the crew shot this scene. The entire shoot occurred in various locations throughout the greater Detroit area, and as anyone familiar with Michigan's climate knows, October night temperatures can be pretty chilly. In the story, the masquerade takes place on a balmy New York evening—July 3, 1776. But during the filming, the low dipped down to an arctic twenty-seven

Costumed partygoers mingle around the refreshment tables.

degrees. As the days of shooting approached, the cold was not the only weather concern. The crew could not shoot in the rain, yet storms loomed on the horizon for days beforehand. Because the party was held after dark, the plan was to shoot for three consecutive nights, but the final night showed such a heavy chance of rain that "we opted to do an extra-long shoot Friday night and into Saturday. Instead of working the typical twelve hours, we would shoot until daylight so we could utilize every hour of darkness that we had," recalls best boy Philip Bolzman. This was a tough decision for the crew to make, because it would force them to complete three nights of work in just two. The crew had already been filming many weeks of night shoots prior to this scene and was running on little sleep. Many were fighting sickness, and the freezing rain and strong winds did little to help. To top it off, the crew would have to pull up to twenty-some hours both nights. The pressure was on.

Despite the grim outlook as they headed into the shoot, there were many clear evidences of God's blessing and grace through the process. The weather turned out to be one of them. With the adjusted two-day schedule, the rain held off. It only rained on one shooting night, pouring for a thirty-minute period that, incredibly, overlapped the crew's lunch break of the same duration. God also provided the unity and stamina the crew needed to be able to do the job. In the director's words, "It would be fair to call the ball the best of times and the worst of times. It was miserable shooting conditions. People were really, really tired. Nerves were stretched and frayed, but at the end of the day, the team really pulled together and really pulled off something that is remarkable. I think it's charming, and it's a fantastic turning point for our story. It's going to do a great job moving the plot forward and moving people emotionally."

DANCE CHOREOGRAPHY

At the center of every proper ball is an elegant dance. The choreography team had to provide something appropriate to the time period as well as to the scene. The challenge of finding a historical line dance in the English contra dance style was that the scene required the main characters to hold an extended dialogue while dancing. This would be simple if the couple were in a waltz position, but the nature of a line dance often separates the couple, sending them a fair distance apart where a private conversation would not be possible. The Duke of Kent's Waltz, with variations from a Russian masquerade, was the solution. Peter Burns, part of the choreography team, explains, "The Duke of Kent's Waltz keeps the couple somewhat close to each other. When you compare other line dances, they stay fairly tight. That would be a good opportunity to get the dialogue in that needed to happen. This dance fit the bill, and it was a beautiful dance—very graceful—so we chose to go with it."

Once the dance was chosen, the scene needed partygoers. There were roughly ninety ball guests needed, and it was quite a demanding job to cast people who looked like wealthy colonists and had the ability to dance. The extras coordinators spent weeks searching their databases and contacting potentials. Costumes also had to be taken into consideration. Although clothes would be tailor-made, the look of each couple had to fit with the theme of their costume.

Once extras were selected, it was time for choreography rehearsals. "All the extras had to go through the training. They were specially taught to make sure they knew what they were doing," says Peter. They needed to know the dance very well, not only so they looked good on camera, but also because, in many cases, their masks hindered their peripheral vision, so they could not easily see their hands or feet during the shoot. To help with the training, several crew members had learned the dance. They were able to mingle with the extras during rehearsals and work individually with them, coaching them on rhythm, form, and steps. "It was quite fun, and also quite confounding, when people had no idea what they were doing. We worked to slowly bring them up out of the mire of confusing steps and turn it into a graceful dance that was appealing to watch," recalls Peter.

On the nights of filming, a speaker system was set up with the music cued. Although there was a string quartet on set, the rhythm the guests were dancing to was prerecorded. A dance instructor was present during the night coaching the extras and calling the dance cues during each take. In the end, all of the preparation paid off. The dance went smoothly, and the extras tirelessly danced all through the night. They had become confident colonial waltzers, and the graceful steps of the Duke of Kent's Waltz blended with the scene to help tell a powerful story.

> "the *center* of every proper ball is an *elegant dance.*"

Charlotte turns to see Will at her arm.

            WILL REYNOLDS
    May I have this dance?

            CHARLOTTE
    Why, I hardly...

He sweeps her onto the dance floor.

            WILL REYNOLDS
    Duke of Kent's Waltz, do you know

"Spacious grounds slate terraces and elegant detailing just right for the *masquerade."*

The stonework on the Scripps grounds made the perfect party setting.

BELOW LEFT: Gray slate tiled the roof.

BELOW RIGHT: This elegant lady, with her blooming iris, belongs to a set of statues on the Scripps lawn that represent the four seasons.

LOCATION SCOUTING

*L*ong before the cameras rolled, years before, in fact, the team was searching for a location for the colonial masquerade. They needed something expansive, elegant, historically appropriate, and available to a film crew. Although several options had been explored, they weren't finding anything. Coincidentally, Andrea, the producer's wife had played her viola for an event at a local mansion many years before. Recalling the site's mysterious, almost magical beauty, she mentioned it as a possible location, and the team decided to look into it.

A welcoming yet impressive estate, Scripps Mansion was built in 1927 by wealthy businessman and newspaper publisher William Scripps. The mansion itself, built in the Tudor style, was perfect to play the English Holloway House, and the spacious grounds with their slate terraces and elegant detailing were just right for the New York mayor's masquerade. The team had found their setting.

The team was pleasantly surprised to learn that the managers of the estate utilized it to facilitate a faith-based ministry and were delighted to open their location to a Christian film. "The Lord really opened the door. We got a tour and felt like it would be a sweet place to hold several of our sets," explains producer Aaron Burns.

The mansion's sixty-seven rooms reveal its intended design as a house for guests and parties. Used for other purposes now, it has been many years since Scripps Mansion's zenith, and many of the grounds were in disrepair when the team arrived. The Scripps managers were gracious in allowing the team to clean up the landscape and make several repairs to the grounds. They restored the stone fountain and prepped the site for a celebration. As Aaron says, "It's what it was designed for, so it was really fun to be able to bring the party back to Scripps Mansion like it might have been back in its heyday."

BELOW: Many of the elaborate masks were imported from Europe.

OPPOSITE: Concept art and final costumes for the Gypsy couple, played by producer Aaron Burns and his wife Andrea.

WARDROBE

"The ball scene itself was wardrobe's greatest challenge. This scene alone had as many costumes as there were main characters' costumes for the rest of the film," lead wardrobe designer Marilyn Burns explains. The elaborate designs and level of detail on the massive number of gowns required hundreds of hours of work. At a masquerade, guests come dressed as various characters or creatures, not unlike a modern costume party. The most important element of the costume is the mask, which is meant to hide the guest's identity from the other partygoers, who have to guess who others really are.

There were twenty featured dancers in the film, in addition to the main characters and other extras. These costumes were the most elaborate of the film and were specially designed by Marilyn.

While the costumes maintained the cut and silhouette of a colonial suit or dress, Marilyn cleverly incorporated elements to represent the characters people were to depict. Each dancer coordinated with his or her partner, and their costumes added depth to the story. For one set of dancers, the lady was a unicorn and the man was a lion. These are traditional symbols of the British Empire: England's coat of arms is supported on either side by a lion and a unicorn. This couple would have been flaunting their loyalty to the crown. Another couple's costumes were made in a nautical theme. The man was dressed as an admiral, but his costume was carefully designed to avoid the colors of both the French and British navies, since this couple was intended to be neutral with regard to independence. The admiral's lady wore a gown with detailing reminiscent of naval knots, and mounted atop her colonial updo was a model ship. As fantastical as it may sound and look, this hairstyle was an actual contemporary fashion. Records exist from the early 1770s of ladies wearing such preposterous items in their hair.

In keeping with the colonial period's fascination with the bizarre, other couples were dressed in costumes influenced by Gypsy, Renaissance, Egyptian, and ancient Greek themes, each representing a piece of history.

The wardrobe team prepared for the ball scene for many weeks beforehand, but due to the tight deadline of casting the main dancer extras and some funding constraints, wardrobe was not able to get the fittings to begin making their costumes until shortly before the ball. Once they had the extras' measurements, several specific pieces of the costumes had to be purchased.

Many of these specialty items had to be ordered from dealers in Europe, India, and across the country. As Marilyn remembers, "The costume pieces were estimated to arrive in five business days, but as the night of the ball

MASQUERADE BALL - **GYPSY COUPLE**

got closer, we were still waiting on ten key items. I made a list of the missing packages, and every time we gathered to pray and plan out our work assignments, we prayed with increasing urgency that they would arrive that afternoon. Throughout the project, the mail truck brought stacks of packages, but we had almost no deliveries at all the entire week before the ball.

"The day shooting for the ball scene began, we had to leave at 2:00 p.m. We were still missing a long list of items, including fine jewelry, shoes, and several Venetian masks. I really didn't have any suitable replacements. At 12:30 p.m., the mail truck stopped in our driveway, and the carrier started making trips to the house. We all ran out with open arms to take the boxes. It was

MASQUERADE BALL - **HENRY & ELIZABETH**

the most faith-building moment of the entire project for me—God showed Himself strong in providing for us. Not a moment early! But just soon enough."

incredible—there were at least a dozen packages, big and small. We stacked all of them on the table, and before we opened anything, we circled around and prayed that what we needed for that night would be in those boxes. There was a flurry of scissors, Bubble Wrap, and packing tape and then shouts of joy as we realized that every single thing on our 'critical' list was in the boxes. That was without a doubt

ABOVE: This couple was dressed as Queen Elizabeth I and King Henry the VIII.

OPPOSITE: (TOP) Inside the honey wagon's hairdressing room, the walls were lined with ready-to-go wigs.

(BOTTOM LEFT) Tanya positions John Rhys-Davies's wig.

(BOTTOM RIGHT) A masquerade dancer's updo, complete with feathers.

HAIR

*T*he hair department had a blast doing their job for the ball. Wardrobe provided the matching masks along with each extra's costume, but it was up to the hair team to come up with the additional pieces to complete each couple's look, and they definitely had some interesting subjects. Hairstyles in the 1770s were quite ostentatious. Key hair artist Tanya Walker was the team's wig expert, and she handmade wigs for several of the main characters and extras. But most of the women's hair had to be made into updos that night. The team did a fantastic job of preparing beforehand, and they were able to process ninety people in about eight hours. Various extras had anything from a horn to an Egyptian serpent worked into their hair. Or how about a bird's nest, a wreath of grapes, or a sailing ship? You never knew what elaborate creation would appear on set next. It was a challenge to secure the items in the extras' hair well enough that they could dance all night without mishap. Once all of the extras had been processed, the team made their way out of the Scripps hair and makeup studio to the set to make adjustments throughout the night. Hairstylist Kristen Hulbert aptly describes the set: "It was neat to come out of the studio and see this gorgeous setting. The set decorators did a beautiful job. The lighting was gorgeous. Even though it was a cold night, the cold did not come through the film. What came through that screen was magical and beautiful." The hair department was a lighthearted and fun team and always seemed to keep the rest of the crew smiling.

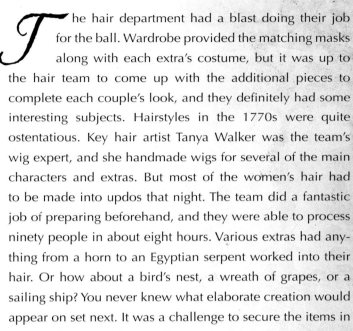

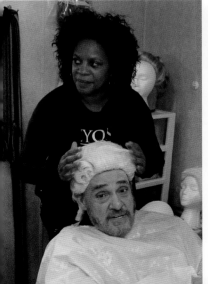

RIGHT: Crew members rig paper lanterns
along the stone wall.

BELOW: Set dresser Adrianne Burns
designed the masquerade party decor.

ART

The masquerade scene was a wealthy eighteenth-century ball, so sophistication and historical accuracy were priorities. The art team lined the stone walls with colonial-style tapestries and paper lanterns to set the mood. Set dresser Adrianne Burns headed up research on colonial party décor: "We decorated with lots of rich materials and food, silver trays, silver table settings, and fresh flowers to give it a historical but elegant look." Much study went into what foods people would have had access to in that location and time in early America. The art team discovered that the colonials decorated with lots of fruits, so they used fruit to add color to the tables' centerpieces. Pineapple was incorporated because it was the colonial symbol for hospitality. Puddings and pastries were very popular party foods, and the tables were laden with these delicacies. But as assistant set dresser Dan Stibral recalls, he had to keep a weather eye on the pastries all night to make sure they did not get eaten!

The art department's job was not over once the decorating was finished, however. Autumn leaves had come down early that year and were blanketing the lawn. Art cleaned the lawn, and there were no leaves present when the set was dressed, but the strong winds that swept the area throughout the nights of shooting were constantly scattering more leaves across the set. Piles of brown leaves would not line the ground in New York in July, so the art team had to vigilantly battle with the wind. The threatening rain also kept the team on their toes. Miraculously, on the nights of shooting, it only rained during lunch break, and it stopped again when the team needed to continue shooting. All of

the tables of food had to be covered while it rained. Dan remembers, "When it was all said and done, it worked out really well. The food was a little soggy, but since none of the extras were actually eating any of it, it was okay."

OPPOSITE: The tables were laden with real fruits and
colonial-style desserts.

FIRE EFFECTS

Playing with fire may seem like an easy job, but being a fire effects wrangler can be a complex job. "In the shots of the ball scene, there are actually five different kinds of fire," explains special effects assistant Aaron Ledden. There were wax candles burning on the tables, fire-log campfires scattered over the stone patios, kerosene torches in the hands of the guards, dehydrated ethanol fire pans on top of the columns, and elevated fire braziers that used a combination of coal, fire logs, and lighter fluid. The special effects team experimented with a variety of fuels to find the correct one for each flame source.

"wax candles, log campfires, torches, fire pans, and elevated fire braziers . . ."

One of the most difficult aspects of the fire effects was the reset process. Each shot of the movie could be filmed multiple times. For the sake of continuity, the scene had to return to the way it was just before the previous take.

OPPOSITE: (LEFT) Aaron Ledden and Dan Stibral kept the candles burning at the right heights all night.

(TOP RIGHT) The warm glow of the firelight added elegance and life to the set.

(MIDDLE) These fire braziers were handmade for the scene.

(BOTTOM RIGHT) The bonfires made a great gathering place between takes. Here several partygoers warm their icy hands while they wait for the next shot.

On take five, the scene should look exactly like it did at the beginning of take one. That meant that all actors had to return to "position one," props had to be returned to their places, and the fires might need to be reset to the correct flame level.

The candles, torches, and fire pans all had a limited lifespan, so conserving them was a concern. When there was a several-minute pause in filming, the team would have to snuff the candles, douse the torches, and extinguish the fire pans. As soon as picture was up again, they would run to relight each one. Additionally, they would have to "rejuice" (add more fuel to) the braziers with lighter fluid or kerosene for an extra burst of flame just before the shot. This was a full-time task for several guys. The most effective tool for extinguishing a fire pan was discovered to be a baking sheet, and throughout the night, the guys could be seen darting between all twenty-five pans either smothering or relighting. The bonus of the job was one of fire's side effects—warmth.

CATERING

More people were present on set for the ball scene than at any other time during production, so catering had a challenging job ahead of them: tirelessly providing three meals a day—or night—for an army of people. Since the crew was filming at Scripps Mansion instead of the production lot, the catering crew was unable to work out of their usual kitchen. Aaron's church, which was just down the road from Scripps, graciously opened their industrial kitchen for food preparation, and the locations team provided two tents to use for serving and dining. Scripps did not have an available kitchen, so catering had to feed their biggest crowd without any facilities (such as sinks or refrigerators) on location. Each day, catering had to pack their supplies into three vehicles and transfer them to set.

Many believers in the area had heard about the Christian movie project and were moved to help out by donating food. The week of the ball, there was a seven-day stretch where every first meal included a donated dish. Head caterer Al Fisher called the donations "a blessing from God." This gave the team a little bit of a reprieve and allowed them to focus on the added complexities of working out of a tent. Although they had two adjoining tents, the number of people involved kept them short on room. Adding to the complexity were the colonial dresses, which had eighteen-inch "pocket hoops" on each side, making movement in the crowded tent a challenge for everyone.

Coffee consumption increased with night shoots—especially when the temperature was below freezing. The crew was getting so little sleep that the caffeine really helped them keep going. It was during the weeks of shooting at Scripps that the catering team started to get creative with their coffee beverages, and soon the crew was able to order several different delicious flavors. The kitchen crew would write personalized messages of encouragement on each cup and run the hot drinks out to the crew on set who could not leave their posts. These efforts helped to raise the morale of the crew. The most popular and legendary of these drinks was a delectable hot cocoa and coffee concoction invented by Joe Henline, one of the production assistants. He labeled his specialty a "HoJo," and the name stuck. The drinks invented those nights at Scripps could be seen stacked three high, being rushed to set every night for the remaining months of production. "On a cold autumn night, Joe with his hands full of custom-made coffee was the lifeblood of the team," says Nathan Burns, property master. "In summary," says Al, "catering made food, hauled food, peddled food, loaded vans, unloaded vans, washed dishes, washed dishes, and washed some more dishes."

"Catering *made* food, *hauled* food, *peddled* food . . . *washed* dishes, *washed* dishes, and *washed* some more *dishes*."

OPPOSITE: (TOP LEFT) Al Fisher prepares a meal at the production office farm house in what became known as "The Little Green Kitchen."
(TOP RIGHT) Joe Henline creates one of his beverage masterpieces.
(BOTTOM) The catering tent offers a warm and inviting glow on a night shoot.

PRODUCTION

Production is the department in charge of keeping people on schedule and making sure things get done in a timely and organized manner. They also take care of the talent. With such a huge group of extras and actors, production was quite busy during the ball scene shoot. Before shooting began, all ninety cast members had a specific time slot to get through hair, makeup, and wardrobe. Production assistants (PAs) did everything they could to keep things running smoothly and efficiently in order for the entire shoot to stay on time. To expedite the process, production divided the hair and makeup departments into four separate units.

Once the cast was ready, the PAs would bring them to set. Not every person was needed for every shot, so they would have to bring the various actors and extras back and forth between their trailers and the set throughout the night. It was during the rainy, frigid ball scene that the PAs discovered a particular feature about the exterior of John Rhys-Davies's trailer—the exhaust pipe. In between their runs, they would take turns huddling around its warmth, trying to thaw their icy fingers.

But the cold affected the cast the most. Unable to dress for the weather, they had to be costumed appropriately for a midsummer's party. Although they wore layers underneath, the stiff wind and twenty-seven-degree air sliced through their silk attire. The production team did their best to keep the cast warm. When there was a long reset, the cast would be escorted back inside, but it took fifteen minutes to get the entire group back and forth from the set. So for shorter periods, the cast had to remain on standby. The production team was prepared with piles of blankets and coats. The contrast between the extras' colonial summer attire and the modern parkas and wool blankets wrapped over top was amusing. When the assistant director made the call to "collect the coats," the PAs would race down the line of extras, gathering all of the incongruous coverings. Immediately after the take was cut, they would reissue the blankets and coats. The main characters had their own assistants to make sure their needs were met. Production assistant Rowan Talmage stayed with Kara Killmer throughout the night to be certain that "she wasn't allowed to go rogue and tough it out. We wanted to make sure that she was actually warm and taken care of," explains second assistant director Peter Burns. The production team stayed busy running back and forth to set all night. Peter admits, "It's a lot of work keeping everyone warm and able to give their peak performance."

> ". . . the **cold** affected the cast the most. Unable to dress for the weather, they had to be costumed . . . for a *midsummer's party*."

OPPOSITE: (TOP) Chad gives Andrew some notes while he warms up with a coffee. (BOTTOM LEFT) Cast and crew mingle on set as the cameras prepare to roll. (BOTTOM RIGHT) Between takes, twentieth-century coats went on over eighteenth-century costumes.

GRIP & ELECTRIC

For G&E (all things power and light), shooting the ball scene presented a challenge because of its scale. The area that had to be lit was massive. Not only the mansion itself, but the entirety of the lawn with all of the layers of the party had to be illuminated. The day of the ball, the G&E guys had to begin setup about five hours before cameras rolled. Their normal supply of lights and gear was not enough for the scene, so they rented extra gear as well as an eighty-foot lift with which to raise the massive 18K light over the top of the mansion. This light played the part of the moon for the scene, and its powerful beam shed a beautiful silver light across the lawn. One of the grips had to man the light from the top of the lift, so Joseph Santoyo spent the entire shoot eighty feet off the ground, only coming down once for lunch break during the twelve-hour shoot. The view was pretty good, but although Joseph never complained about it, the wind was bitter at that height, and the only source of warmth was the small amount of heat radiating from the light.

Even with the additional lights, the team was cutting it close on having enough equipment. In the words of best boy Philip Bolzman, "We were pretty much maxing out our entire package the night of the ball. All of our lights, all of our extension cords, everything but the generator. It was fun to be running at full capacity. It's a good feeling. You know you're giving it all you've got. There's nothing left in reserve." Another large light was staged on a twenty-foot scaffolding, and several times throughout the night when the camera changed direction to film the other side of the

set, G&E had to move the rig. This was quite a process and required the effort of several men.

The finer details that G&E incorporated gave the scene more depth. The G&E guys worked with the art team to create the paper lanterns that lined the area behind the dancers, giving the scene an additional glow of warmth. And by placing lights inside the mansion, they also added a fun touch to the story, as lighting technician Joshua Hedrick explains: "It added some nice depth to the imagery and made it appear like the party was continuing inside." In the end, their labors paid off with incredible results. The lighting of the ball scene completed the magical touch that each department had been striving to achieve.

OPPOSITE: (TOP) The G&E team always had their gear, apple boxes, sandbags, and lights ready to go.
(BOTTOM LEFT) Joseph Santoyo on the ground again beside the eighty-foot lift.
(BOTTOM RIGHT) Several of the grips in their truck. Left to right: Josh Hedrick, Tim Jones, Andrew Hurt, and Nathaniel Brunner.

RIGHT: Josh Hedrick receives directions over his walkie-talkie as he adjusts a light.

CAMERA

While every other part of the crew worked to create some part of the scene, the camera department actually captured it for the movie. On a film set, each moment is precious. And on the last night of the masquerade shoot, the camera team was in a literal race against time. "We had an enormous amount of shots we were trying to get on a very tight schedule, and we had to get it all filmed before the sun rose," says assistant cameraman Alex Lerma. The task before them was daunting.

Planned into the ball scene were many visually creative and beautiful shots. These added beauty to the film but also took time to execute. There were several complicated crane shots, such as the top-down view of the dance, as well as several Steadicam shots. A Steadicam is a camera stabilization system that produces a smooth look while the camera operator is walking or running. First assistant cameraman Jonathan Hedrick, whose job it was to manually focus the Red Scarlet camera, talks about the setup. "We had one shot of John Rhys-Davies coming down the stairs with a really crazy focus pull. I had to wrack focus from a moving Steadicam as it maneuvered through the crowd." Jonathan would typically focus the lens from a remote monitor using a wireless device, but because the camera was moving through a crowd of people, this was not an option. Jonathan had to focus the shot directly off of the moving camera without seeing the image. "It was just a matter of judging and gauging the distance. It was a blast."

No one had counted on the effects of subfreezing temperatures on the equipment. Recalling his struggle against the elements, Jonathan elaborates, "Your hands do this cramp deal. And the lenses get really cold, so that makes it even harder to focus, because the rotation of the lens gets more difficult."

But lenses are not the only piece of equipment the cold can impact. Unbeknownst to the team, the Red camera batteries they had been cycling through over the night were not receiving any charge from the power units. The cold had caused the chargers to malfunction. Not until the last battery was dead did they discover the error. The battery chargers were immediately relocated to thaw, and the cameras began running on backups. Alex remembers the situation: "Just a few minutes before dawn, we were racing to get our last shot. I remember sitting behind the camera watching the battery meter count down and trying to calculate if we were actually going to have enough battery to finish the shoot. If we ran out, everything that the whole team did to bring this ball scene together would have been for naught. That was intensely stressful for me. I vividly remember that. But the sun rose, mercifully, and we had a few minutes left on our last battery." As the crew finished the last shot of the night, the orange glow of the sunrise could clearly be seen brightening the eastern sky. The race against the clock had ended, and the team had successfully completed the shoot.

OPPOSITE: John Rhys-Davies awaits the call of "Action!"
RIGHT: The camera extends over the dancers for a top-down shot.

The Studio

Photo by: VeLoie Alling

PREVIOUS PAGE: The crew crowds around the camera to review the shot of Will's stunt double jumping through the sugar glass window. ABOVE: The members of the Burns family who attended the *Beyond the Mask* premiere: (Left to Right) Nathan, Marilyn, Andy, Tracey, Andrea, Aaron, Chad, Angela, Adrianne, Eleanor, Ray, Shannon, Sara, Nick, and Hannah.

Cousins Chad and Aaron Burns began their journey as filmmakers when they were quite young. Both from homeschool families, they were instilled with a love of history, imagination, and creative storytelling very early in life. Chad was raised in Illinois and Aaron grew up in Michigan, but despite the distance, their families often took advantage of holidays and summer vacations to spend time together.

Their moviemaking journey began when Chad and Aaron recorded their first short film with a shoulder-mounted VHS camcorder. The film starred several of the younger Burns siblings in a superhero duel. "From then on we used our family holidays to create short films," Aaron explains. "At the time we didn't have a desire to make features. It was really just a hobby. But it grew as we did, and in my first year in college, we decided to make a feature film called *Pendragon*.

"It was then that the Lord started to work in our hearts, and we really began to see the power of film. As you read through history and literature, you can see how writers have influenced generations. Although the characters were created hundreds of years ago, these stories are still alive and continue influencing our culture today. It's incredible!

ABOVE: Aaron (dressed as Artos Pendragon) and Chad review a shot on the set of their first feature film, *Pendragon*.

God has given Chad and I, and our families, a desire to tell stories that are fun, that are entertaining, and that are adventurous. And at their heart and woven through them is a message of hope and redemption through a relationship with Jesus Christ."

"We call ourselves Burns Family Studios," Chad says. "The entire Burns family has been involved in making the films, but we also mean the term 'family' in the largest sense of the word, because we have a filmmaking family that spans the entire country and multiple continents now."

It took hundreds of people coming together to produce *Beyond the Mask*. Many of these were young volunteers eager to make a difference in the world around them. For them, *Beyond the Mask* was an opportunity to be a part of something bigger than themselves.

Chad credits his family's homeschool background with the way he and Aaron structure their filmmaking teams: "Homeschooling is a vertically integrated effort. Unlike a standard educational environment, where everybody is segregated by grades, homeschooling is more of a one-room schoolhouse approach. And I think we bring that to the filmmaking endeavor. Burns Family Studios is a very vertically integrated studio. We have people of different ages, people of different aptitudes, people from different parts of the world, and people of different skill levels that have all come together to achieve a common goal."

The lives Chad and Aaron live naturally impact not only those who view their movies, but also the people involved in making them. "I've worked on other projects where Christianity was more of a side thing," a crew member comments, "but with Chad and Aaron, there was always an emphasis that

ABOVE: On days off, the crew enjoyed hanging out together. Here they stop for a picture after going ice skating.

we were making a film for God's glory. That really helped us keep a clear vision of why we were there and what we were doing."

For Chad and Aaron and their team, the goal in life is not to create a great name or be recognized by the world but to bring honor to God. Their relationship with God is a living, visible part of their lives. When asked about his experince with the film, Ade M'Cormack, who plays Joshua Brand, replied that what touched him the most were the people working behind the scenes. "How kind they were, how gracious they were, how magnanimous they were. I just loved their spirit. I had never met people like this before who were so beautiful inside and out. And that touched me so deeply. I remember I called my manager and said, 'You know, these guys are really special, and they've got something special going on here.'"

Aaron explains their motivation: "Even our culture knows that money, possessions, power, fame, whatever it might be that we pursue, ultimately comes up empty. Our hearts' desire is to point people to the hope that we find in a relationship with Jesus Christ. Because there is nothing else in life that can satisfy us."

OPPOSITE: (BOTTOM LEFT) The honey wagon is the term for this trailer. The hair and makeup departments each had a separate space as well as each of the main actors. This was a central hub for the actors and production team. (BOTTOM RIGHT) Crew members filling in as colonial soldier extras strike "plastic army men" poses.

John Rhys-Davies commended the crew for being an energetic team of professional young people. Three months on a film set created a close-knit community.

ABOVE: (LEFT) Stephen Higginbotham records actor arrival and departure times from set. (MIDDLE) Here, Tim Holmes and Seth Rice work together in the art department. (RIGHT) The boom mic was always hovering just outside the camera's frame in the steady hands of boom operator Ferrick Hallaron.

Aaron Burns
CONCLUSION

It's NOT what you do that defines you.

In many ways, *Beyond the Mask* is thematically similar to other films in the "superhero" genre—a heroic character dons a mask to become a vigilante, fighting against crime in an effort to save a city from destruction. But at its heart, this story is fundamentally different. In *Batman Begins*, for example (one of my favorite movies), when Batman is talking to Rachel Dawes just before the climactic battle for Gotham City, he recalls her line: "It's not who I am underneath, but what I do that defines me."

This thought is one that pervades our culture—you are defined by what you accomplish. We are driven by performance: at school, at home, at work, at church. In order to achieve happiness in this world, we have to do. We strive to earn the right to be special, to be loved, to be accepted. It becomes a never-ending task of self-justification and personal redemption.

In a pivotal conversation in *Beyond the Mask*, Charlotte tells Will that "neither redemption nor love can ever be earned; they are gifts granted freely from the heart of God." As simple as this truth is, it is often so easy to get it backwards. God accepts us, not because of what we have done, but because of the righteousness that Christ has earned on our behalf. This is good news.

Blessings in the Heavenly Realm

During filming, our team studied through the first two chapters of Ephesians, exploring some of these ideas in more de-

tail. This passage tells us that our hearts' deepest needs are fulfilled in Him. In Christ, we are: Chosen. Adopted. Made alive. Given grace. For His pleasure. No longer outsiders. Divinely empowered. Promised an inheritance. To the praise of His glory.

Not the End, but the Beginning

These truths have made a significant impact on my life personally and are largely the motivation behind the production of *Beyond the Mask*. As we close this phase of our journey, it's our prayer that these truths that impacted our hearts would come alive for you as well.

I encourage you to search out the divine redemption and love that are found in the heart of God. Look to Him for your continued justification in this life, and place your hope firmly in the wonderful relationship we'll enjoy with Him in eternity someday.

Until next time,

Aaron Burns

All I Have Is Christ

I once was lost in darkest night
Yet thought I knew the way
The sin that promised joy and life
Had led me to the grave
I had no hope that You would own
A rebel to Your will
And if You had not loved me first
I would refuse You still

But as I ran my hell-bound race
Indifferent to the cost
You looked upon my helpless state
And led me to the cross
And I beheld God's love displayed
You suffered in my place
You bore the wrath reserved for me
Now all I know is grace

Now, Lord, I would be Yours alone
And live so all might see
The strength to follow Your commands
Could never come from me
Oh Father, use my ransomed life
In any way You choose
And let my song forever be
My only boast is You

Hallelujah! All I have is Christ
Hallelujah! Jesus is my life

ABOVE: Crew members sing and worship together.

STORIES FROM THE BTM SET:
CREW BIBLE STUDIES
- A Time to Be Still -

During preproduction, Chad and Aaron set up a Bible study on Sunday evenings as a time for the crew to come together and discuss the film's theme—finding your identity in Christ. Aaron and Chad alternated leading the discussions each week as the crew worked through *Counterfeit Gods*, Timothy Keller's outstanding book on the topic. The Bible studies quickly became a favorite time of the week for many, and they gave the team an opportunity to refocus and worship together as brothers and sisters in Christ. The studies built a powerful unity of spirit within the crew. Singing was always a treasured part of these studies, and several crew members would bring out instruments and lead the group in song. "All I Have Is Christ" quickly became the crew's theme song and was sung at every gathering.

Dear Reader, ————

It is our prayer that this book will allow you to join us on the adventure God set before our family and hundreds of friends who worked together to produce *Beyond the Mask*. It is our passion to tell the stories of what God is doing in His creation, and this film gave us a special opportunity to do that. On freezing nights when the team gathered around heaters during breaks; on early mornings when the cast and crew shared a hasty breakfast while the sun rose; or on beautiful fall afternoons when hundreds of extras snaked their way around the set in prearranged patterns; we strove to capture the heart of the moment. We want our photos and stories to bring you to our set to experience our joys and sorrows with us. If you have seen that this film was more than actors and effects—that it was a group of like-minded people striving together to create art that brings glory to God—we will have achieved our goal.

————————

NOT TO US, O LORD, NOT TO US, BUT TO YOUR NAME GIVE GLORY.

PSALM 115:1 ESV

LEFT TO RIGHT: Authors Sara and Shannon Burns.

Cousins Sara and Shannon Burns have been working as professional photographers for six years and have traveled widely expressing their passion through photography. Their first co-written book, *Pendragon: Journey Behind the Scenes*, was released in 2009 as a companion to Burns Family Studios' film *Pendragon: Sword of His Father*.